Language Arts
Workbook A

Siegfried Engelmann

Karen Davis

Jean Osborn

Evan Haney

Acknowledgments

The authors are grateful to the following people for their assistance in the preparations of Reading Mastery Transformations Grade 1 Language.

Cally Dwyer
Katherine Gries
Debbi Kleppen
Patricia McFadden
Piper VanNortwick

mheducation.com/prek-12

Copyright © 2021 McGraw-Hill Education

All rights reserved. No part of this publication may be reproduced or distributed in any form or by any means, or stored in a database or retrieval system, without the prior written consent of McGraw-Hill Education, including, but not limited to, network storage or transmission, or broadcast for distance learning.

Send all inquiries to:
McGraw-Hill Education
8787 Orion Place
Columbus, OH 43240

ISBN: 978-0-07-905561-3
MHID: 0-07-905561-3

Printed in the United States of America.

1 2 3 4 5 6 7 8 9 LMN 24 23 22 21 20

Name _____

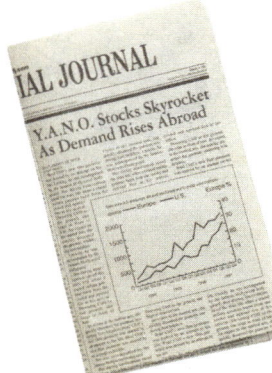

Side 1

Name _____

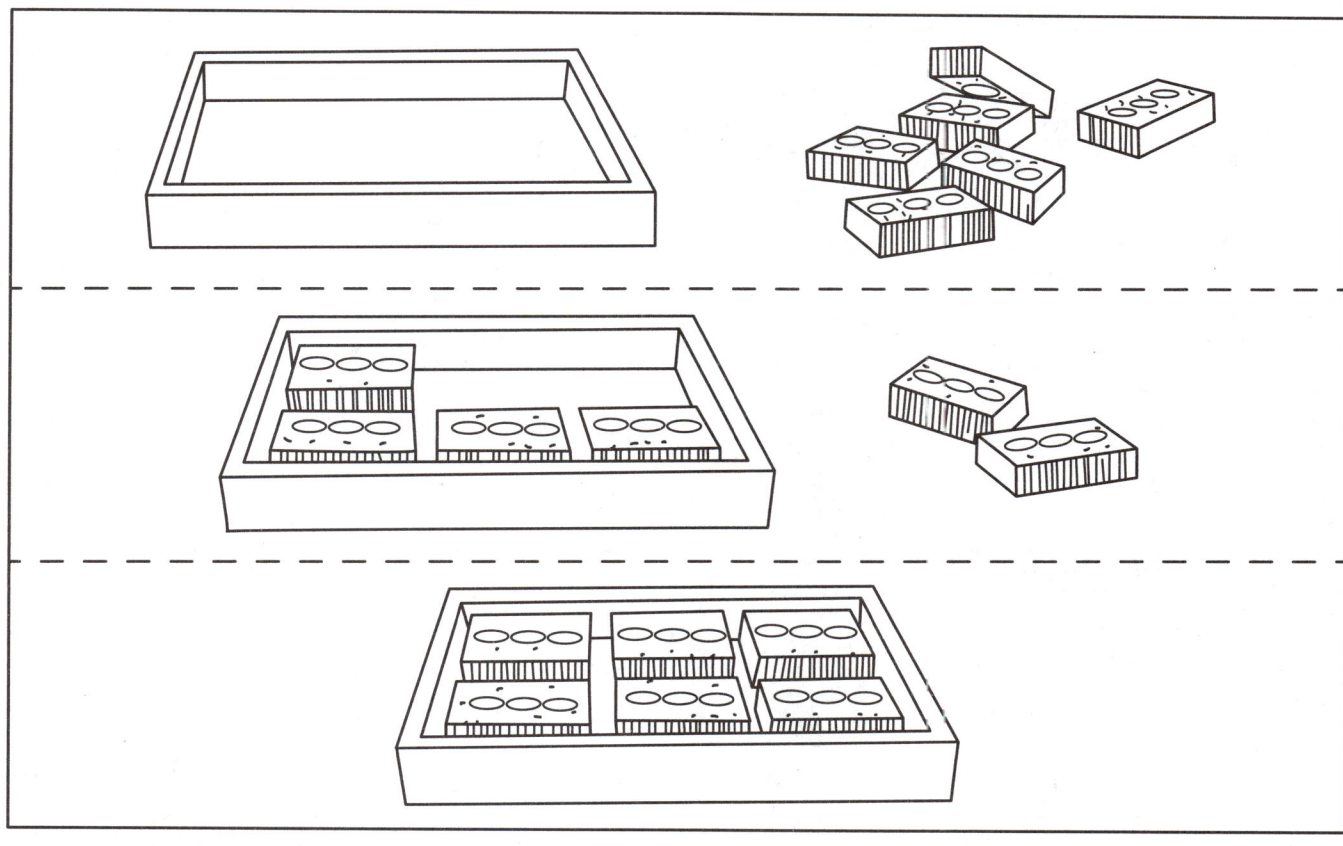

Side 1

Name _____

3

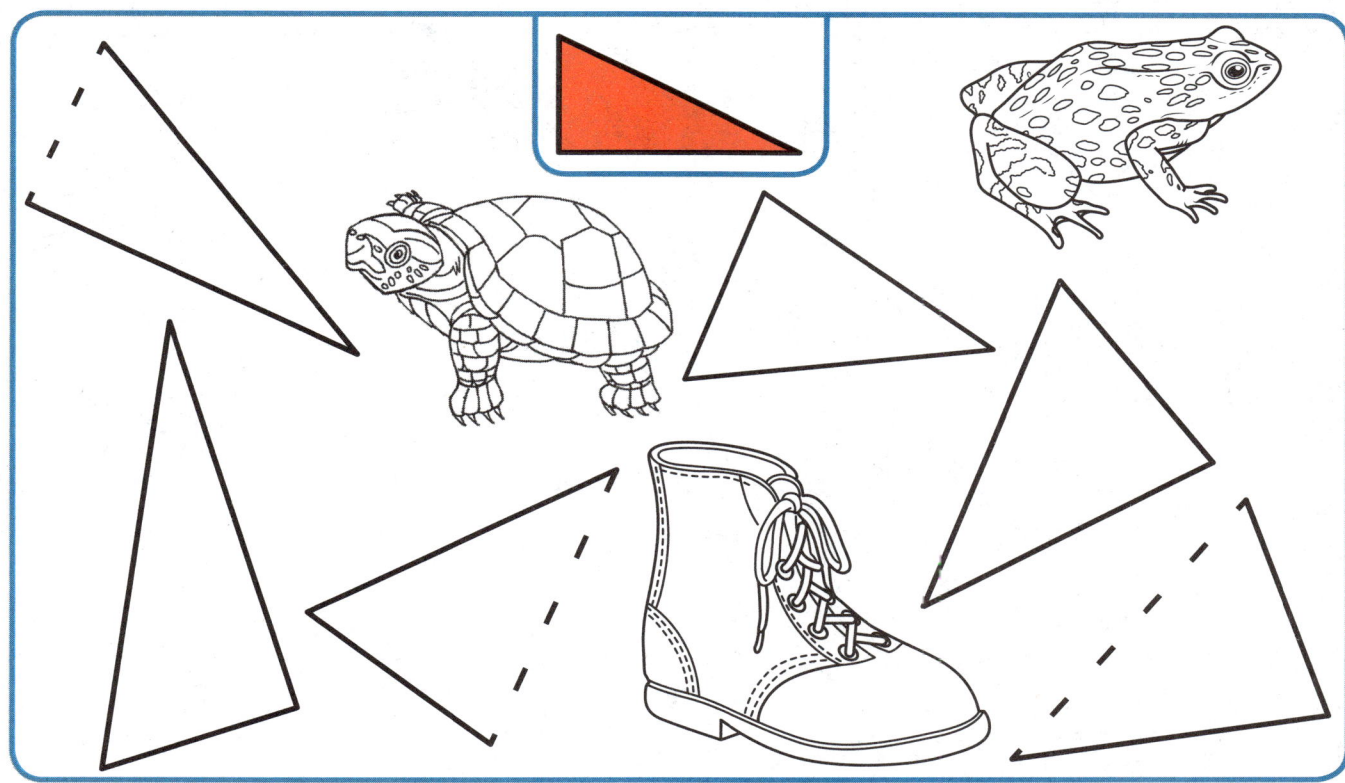

Side 1

Name _____

4

Side 1

Side 2

Name _____

5

Side 1

Name

Side 2

Name

7

Side 1

Side 2

Name

Side 1

Side 2

Name _____

9

Side 1

Side 2

Name _____

10

Side 1

Side 2

Name _____

tools   plants

 _____

 _____

 _____

 _____

| Sunday | Monday | Tuesday | Wednesday |

Side 1

The fox had a bone.

The ram

Name _____

| 12 |

food   vehicles

 _____

 _____

 _____

 _____

| Sunday | Monday | Tuesday | Wednesday |

_____
_____
_____
_____
_____

Side 1

Side 2

The fox had a cake.

The ram

Name _____

| animals | clothing |

 _____  _____

 _____  _____

 _____  _____

| Thursday | Friday | Saturday |

_____

_____

_____

Side 1

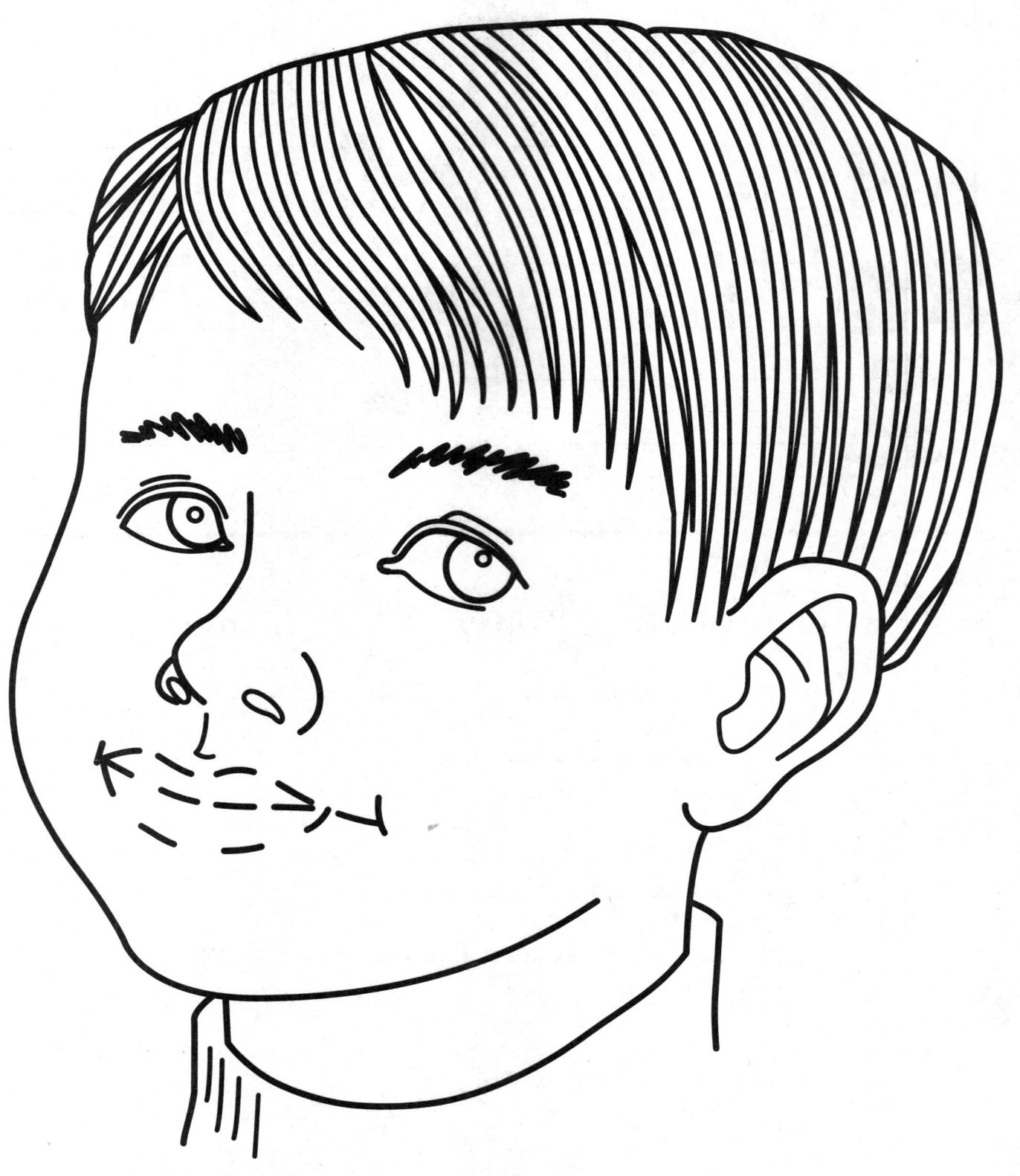

Side 2

The fish is under a boat.
The bird

Name

| rough | tall | old | pull |

1. push _____ 3. smooth _____

2. young _____ 4. short _____

| Thursday | Friday | Saturday |

Side 1

Side 2

The man had a bat.

The ram

Name

15

Sunday Monday Tuesday Wednesday
Thursday Friday Saturday

Side 1

The car is on a road.
The bug

| win | dry | short | fast |

1. slow _____   3. wet _____

2. lose _____   4. tall _____

Side 3

Name

16

Side 1

| big | win | push | smooth | open |

1. rough _____   4. pull _____

2. lose _____   5. small _____

3. shut _____

Side 2

Name _____

| buildings | plants |

 _____  _____

 _____  _____

 _____  _____

Sunday   Monday   Tuesday   Wednesday
Thursday   Friday   Saturday

Side 2

socks   gloves   shoes

His feet had socks.

Her feet

Name _____

| fat | big | long | open | full |

1. empty _____   4. short _____

2. skinny _____   5. small _____

3. shut _____

Side 1

Name

| containers | furniture |

Sunday   Monday   Tuesday   Wednesday
Thursday   Friday   Saturday

Side 2

The bird is on a van.

The bug

Name _____

| clean | lose | fast | sick | open |

1. well _____ 4. slow _____

2. win _____ 5. dirty _____

3. shut _____

| Sunday | Monday | Tuesday | Wednesday |
| Thursday | Friday | Saturday | |

Side 1

Side 2

Name _____

1. Did i eat cake?

2. did you eat cake?

3. i did eat cake.

4. her brother and i have fun.

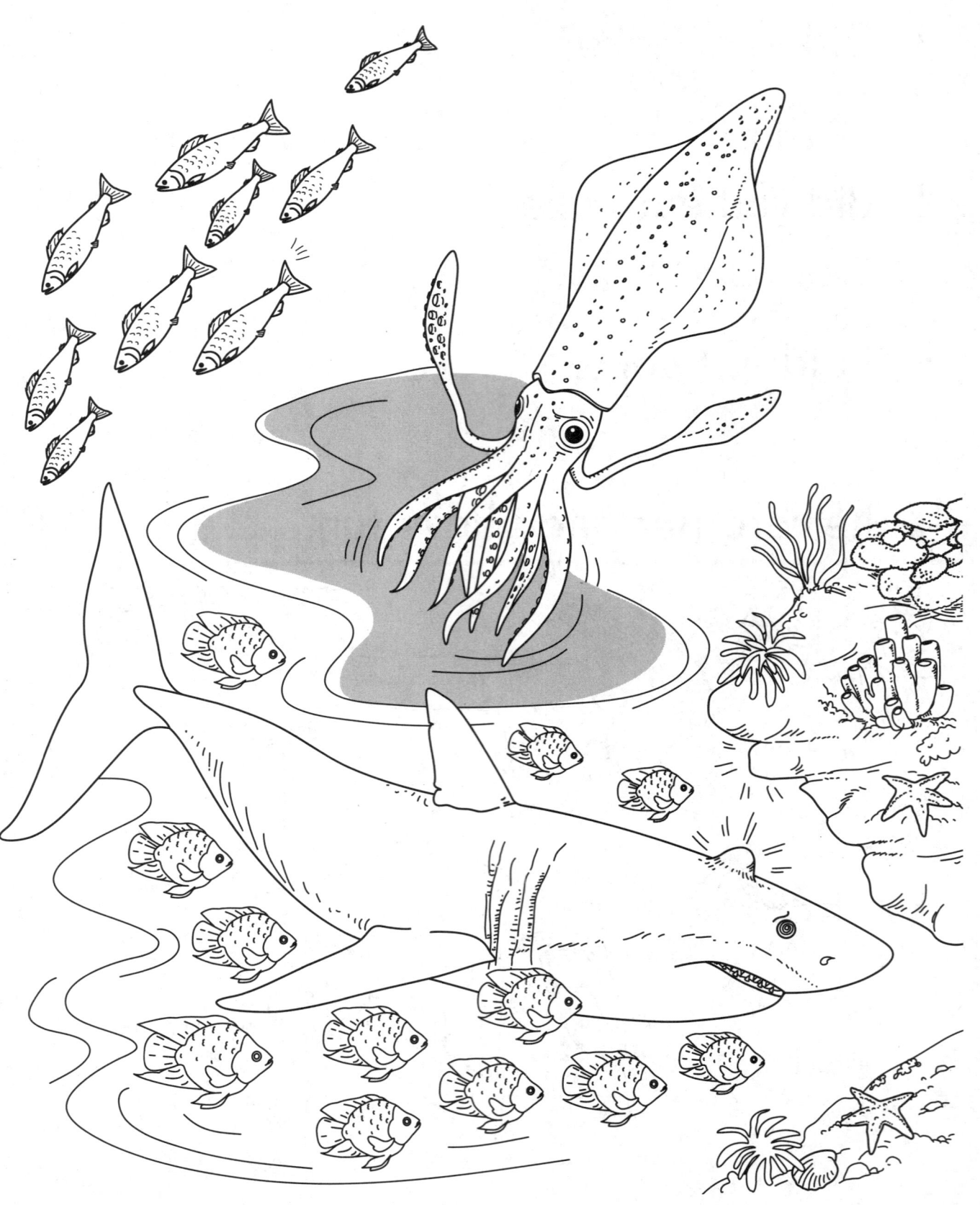

Side 2

Name _____

1. should we help those little children?

2. my mother and i helped those little children.

3. i asked my mother to help those little children.

4. those little children were happy.

Side 1

Side 2

The mole is under a goat.
The rat

Name _____

1. His name was john smith.

2. eddie and his sister vera lived next door.

3. The oldest boy was kurt madison.

4. jim, dan, and sara were in the same class.

| late | awake | soft | noisy | empty |

1. quiet _____   4. early _____

2. full _____   5. hard _____

3. asleep _____

| Sunday | Monday | Tuesday | Wednesday |
| Thursday | Friday | Saturday |

Side 2

Name _____

1. his name is bob wilson.

2. cally and her dog rover are going with ted.

3. is her sister older than mike?

4. debra and i will be late to sam's party.

| animals | vehicles |

Side 1

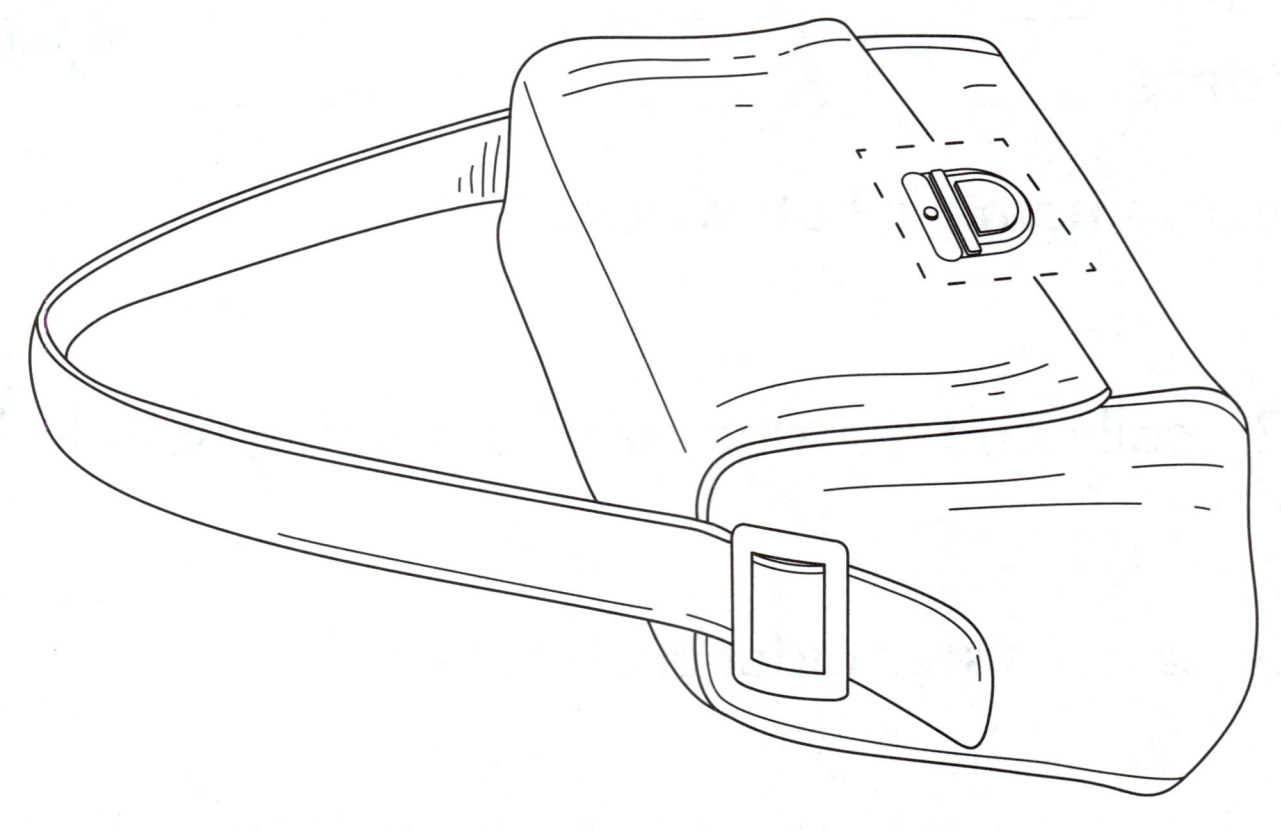

Side 2

Name _____

winter   spring   summer   fall

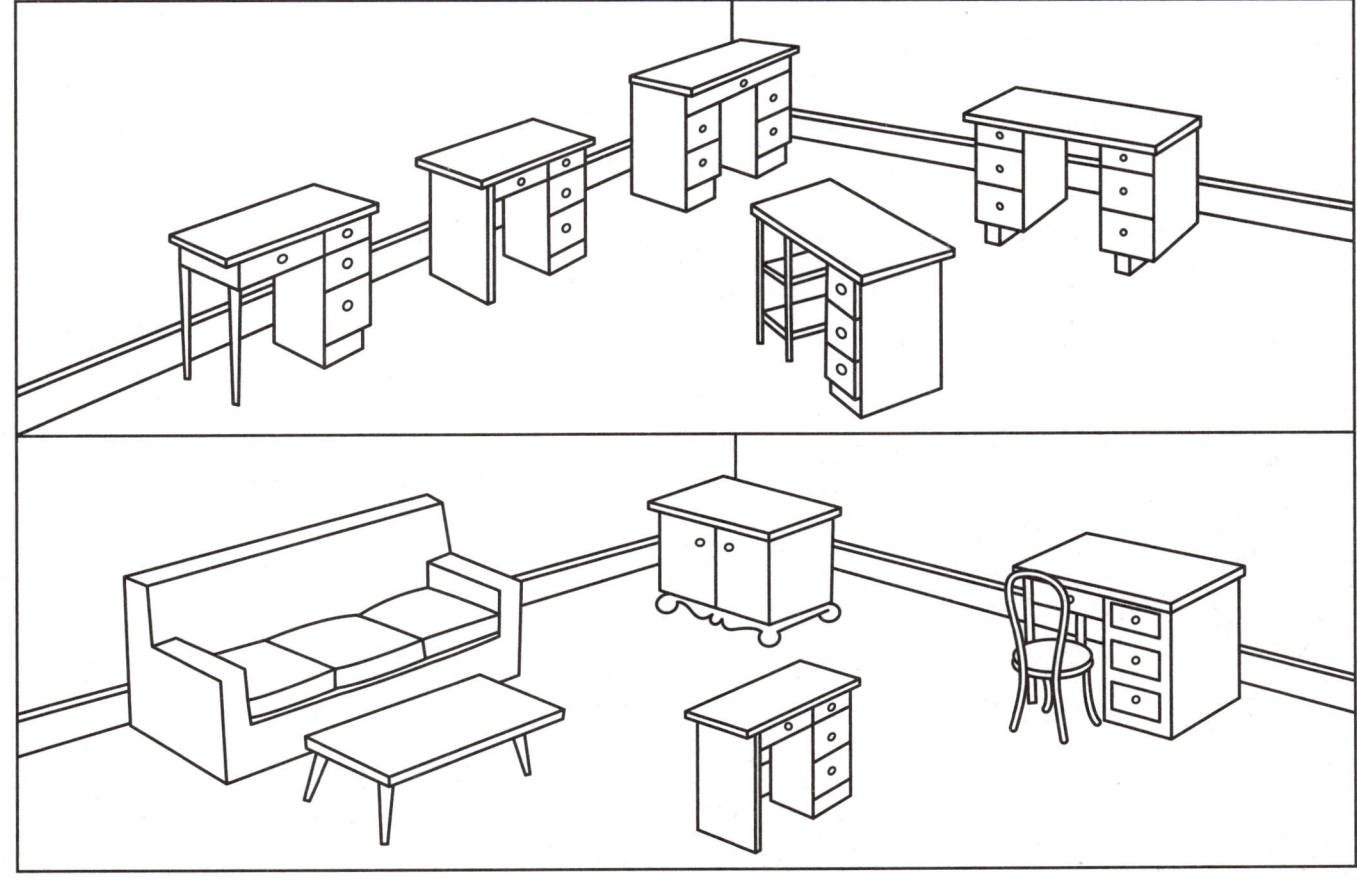

Side 1

Side 2

Name _____

26

1. The king did not like all the _____ that were in the palace.

   | cats | dogs | horses | mice | snakes |

2. The king sent a guard out to find the best _____ in the land.

   | cat | dog | horse | mice | snake |

3. What was the name of the black cat that came to the palace?

   | James | King | Lester | Guard |

Side 1

4. How many mice did Lester catch his first day in the palace?

| 10 | 15 | 20 | 25 | 30 |

5. One mouse thought it would be a good idea to burn down the _____ .

| shed | house | bedroom | palace | kitchen |

6. One mouse thought it would be a good idea to put a _____ around Lester's neck.

| tie | bell | sock | necklace | scarf |

7. Did the wise old mouse think that this plan would work?

| Yes | No |

8. Did the plan work?

| Yes | No |

Side 2

1. will dan and rita come to the party

2. my mom told me that i can play outside

3. her name is li chen

4. do you know where ana went

| winter | spring | summer | fall |

Name _____

1. maria and i will walk to school

2. am i older than you

3. will you call tom davis on the phone

4. we will wait for bill and his friend

| winter | spring | summer | fall |

The ant is in a cake.

The goat

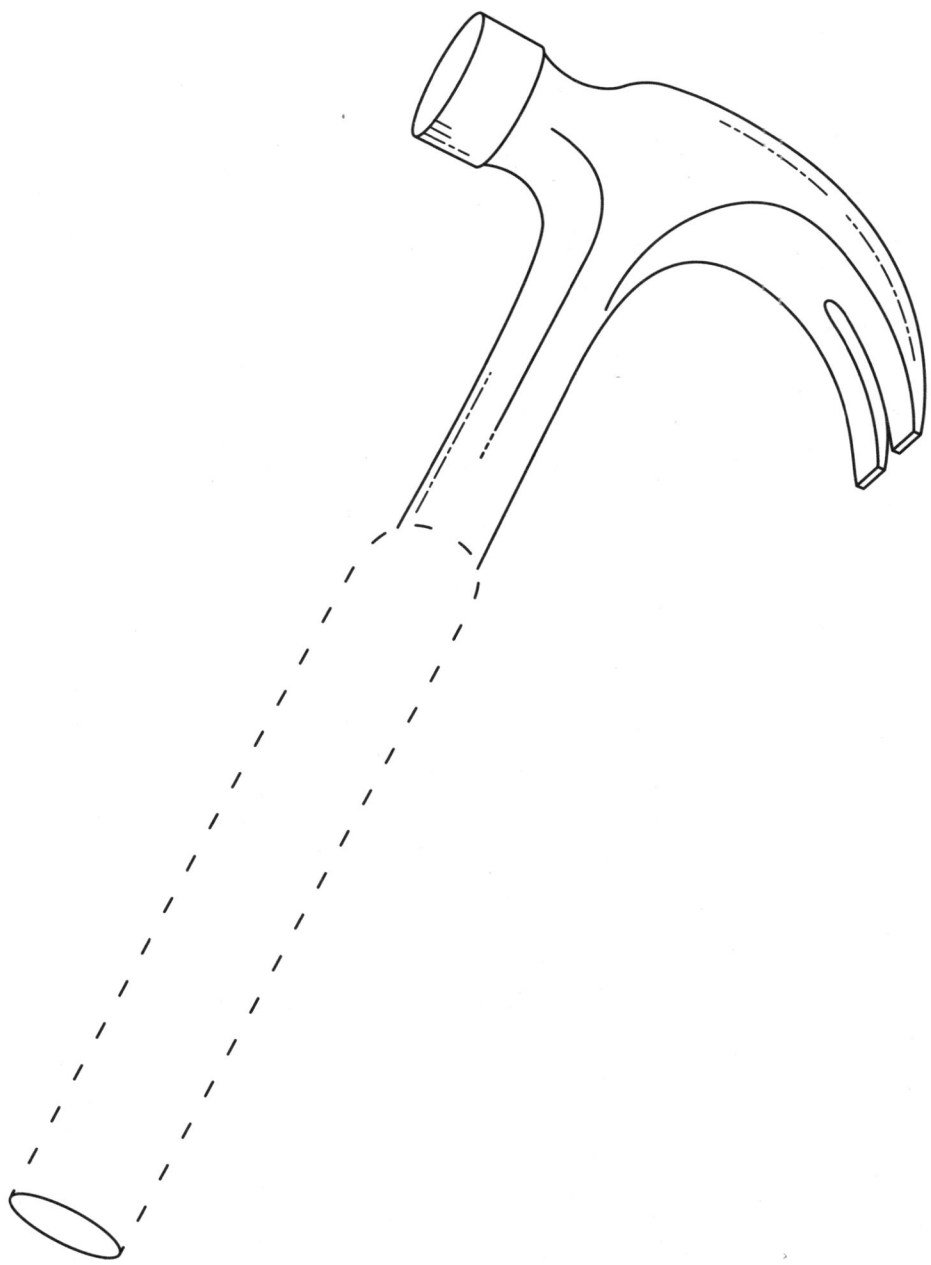

Side 3

Name _____

28

Sunday   Monday   Tuesday   Wednesday
    Thursday   Friday   Saturday

Side 1

| small | short | early | hard |

1. late _____

3. big _____

2. tall _____

4. soft _____

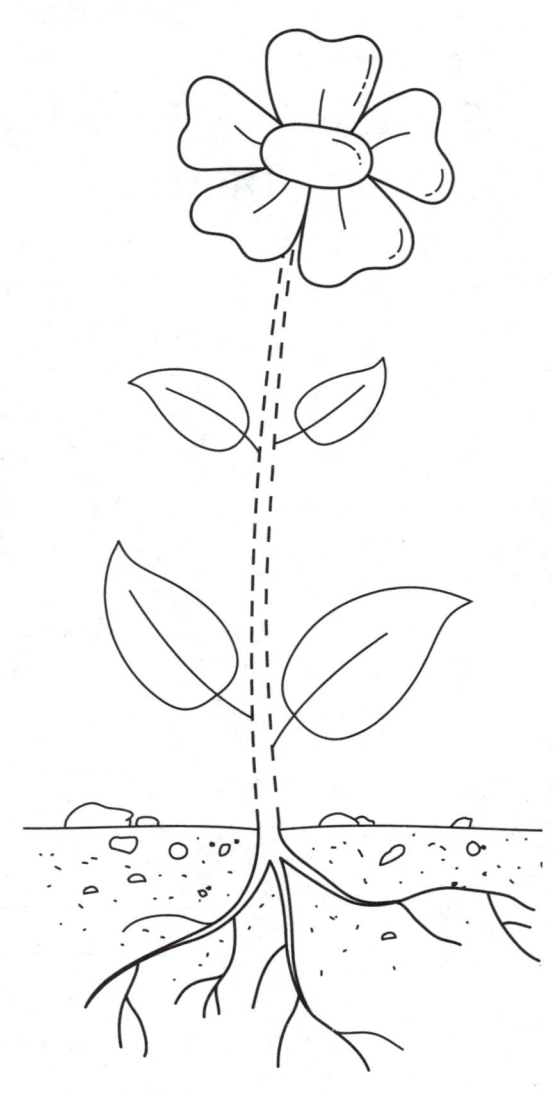

Side 2

Name _____

| winter | spring | summer | fall |

_____
- - - - - - - - - - - - -
_____
- - - - - - - - - - - - -
_____
- - - - - - - - - - - - -
_____
- - - - - - - - - - - - -
_____

Side 1

food	tools

Side 2

Name _____

30

Side 1

rough   young   push   smooth   old   pull

1. The ice was very smooth.

2. One old tree is next to the house.

Side 2

Name _____

31

Side 1

| dry | win | slow | wet | fast | lose |

1. There were wet clothes on the line.

2. The horse was fast.

Name _____

32

1. That man will buy milk ham and cheese.

2. Your dogs ran barked and played.

3. His brother saw lions tigers and birds.

Side 1

The man will sing.

The clock

Side 3

Name _____

1. Nell ate fish salad and corn for dinner.

2. The black cat chases mice birds and bugs.

3. We will buy pens pencils and paper.

| deep | quiet | noisy | raw | shallow | cooked |

1. The children were quiet.
   _____
   _____

2. The water was deep.
   _____
   _____

Side 2

Name _____

1. we saw men boys and dogs

2. did they look at books and pictures

3. she learned to read write and sing

| | True | False |

1. Tables have legs. _____

2. Water is wet. _____

3. Birds have feet. _____

| winter | spring | summer | fall |

_____

Name _____

1. fish live in rivers lakes and ponds

2. my dogs ran and played

3. they looked at houses and barns

4. are the girls boys and men in the store

5. the walls were white pink or gray

	True	False

1. A tree grows in the clouds. _____

2. The sun shines at night. _____

3. A plant is a vehicle. _____

| dull | crying | hard | shiny | easy | laughing |

1. Is that girl crying?

_____

2. We were done with that hard job.

_____

Side 2

Name _____

36

1. The setting of the story about Cindy is _____ .

| an ocean | a forest | a palace | a farm |

2. The shark bonked his head on _____ .

| a ship | the ground | a rock | a door |

3. At the end of the story, the shark thought he was _____ .

| a squid | a fish | a shark | a whale |

4. The setting of the story about Lester is _____ .

| an ocean | a forest | a palace | a farm |

5. The _____ wanted Lester to catch mice.

| shark | pig | king | queen |

Side 1

6. A little mouse put a bell on a ribbon around Lester's _____ .

| leg | arm | tail | neck |

7. The setting of the poem about the frogs is _____ .

| an ocean | a forest | a palace | a farm |

8. There were _____ frogs sitting on the log.

| 10 | 12 | 14 | 16 |

9. At the end of the poem, the frogs were sitting on _____ .

| the log | the ground | Hog | a tree |

True   False

1. A plant is a vehicle. _____

2. Glasses are made of wood. _____

3. A horse can walk. _____

Side 3

Name _____

37

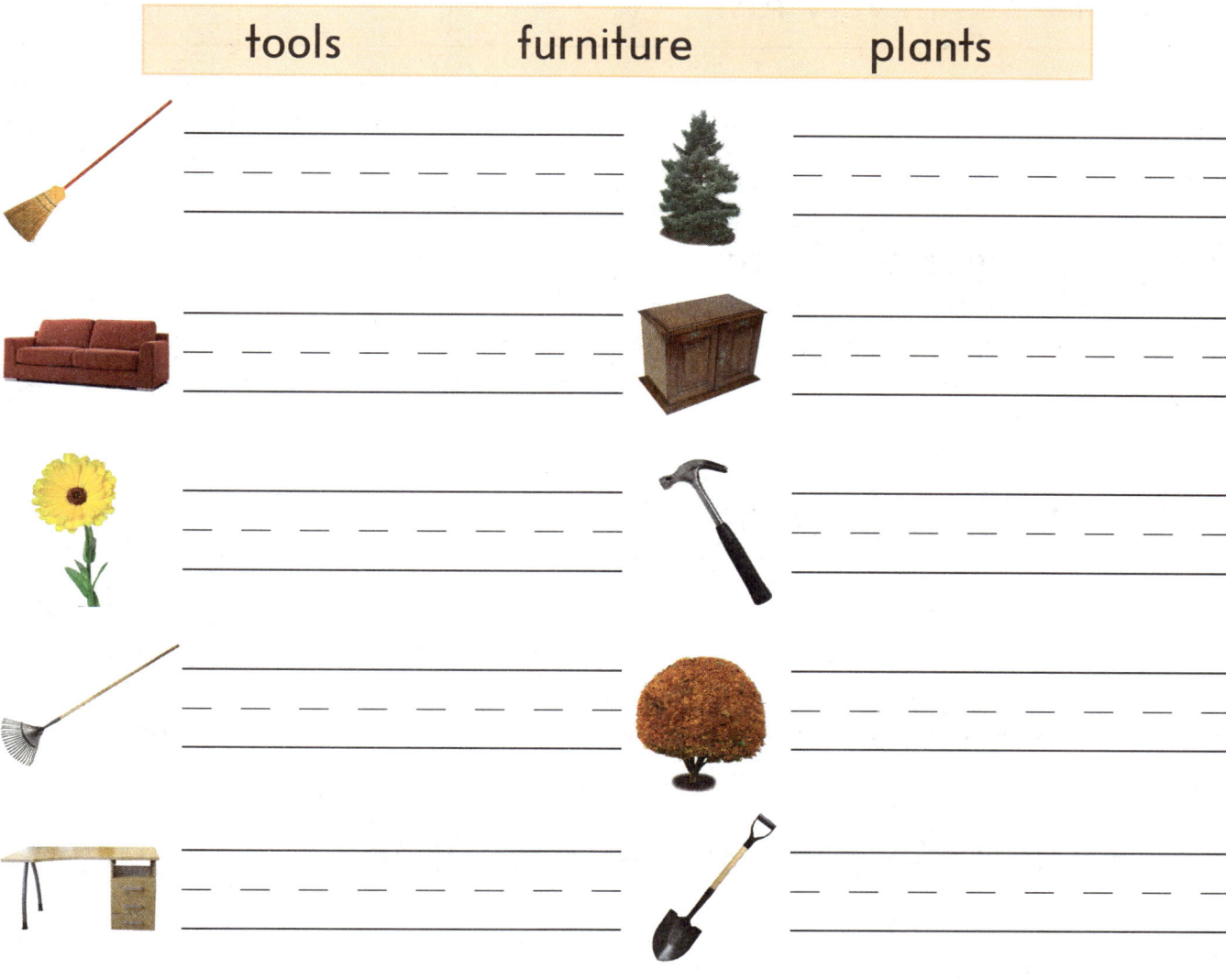

| tools | furniture | plants |

shut   skinny   below   happy   big

1. thin _____   3. closed _____

2. large _____   4. under _____

Side 1

cold   dirty   noisy   slow   awake   narrow

1. The fish swam very fast.

2. My red shoes are clean.

3. Mike will be asleep soon.

---

1. that tree has green brown and yellow leaves

2. my dad said that i can go with tim

3. will maria buy apples grapes and lemons at the store

Side 2

Name _____

38

1. Pat _____
bike

2. Jill _____
house

3. Ann _____
book

4. Bill _____
dog

5. Ken _____
coat

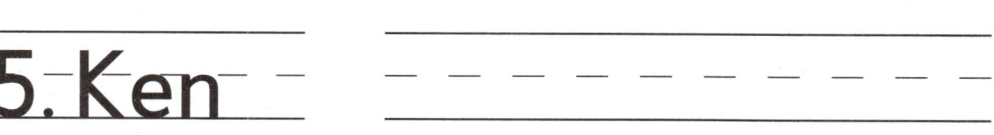
thin   quiet   over   under   small

1. above _____   3. below _____

2. skinny _____   4. little _____

Side 1

| winter | spring | summer | fall |

_____
- - - - - - - - - - - - - - -
_____
- - - - - - - - - - - - - - -
_____
- - - - - - - - - - - - - - -
_____
- - - - - - - - - - - - - - -
_____

Name _____

1. a small boy _____
toy

2. the horse _____
saddle

3. the girl _____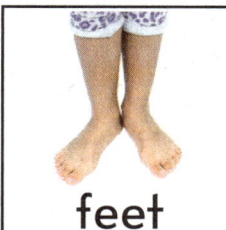
feet

4. the house _____
roof

| healthy | large | below | little | wet |

1. big _____   3. small _____

2. well _____   4. under _____

Side 1

| True | False |

1. A dog barks. _____

2. People eat vehicles. _____

3. You sweep with a broom. _____

---

1. the bike the car and the truck are in the street

2. he ate carrots and cake when i went home

3. do you want bob to wash plates cups and forks

Side 2

Name _____

1. a dog

2. a lady

3. my sister

4. the duck

tail
closet
shoes
beak

| wide | empty | soft | narrow | hard | full |

1. We went down a narrow street.

2. The old chair was soft.

	True	False

1. A train is furniture. _____

2. You can read a bicycle. _____

3. People smell with ears. _____

	animals	plants	food

Side 2

Name _____

1. The setting of the story is a _____.

| lake | ocean | forest | field |

2. The story begins in the _____.

| fall | winter | spring | summer |

3. The story ends in the _____.

| fall | winter | spring | summer |

4. The grasshopper feels _____ when the story begins.

| happy | sad | afraid | bored |

5. Then he feels _____ when the winter comes.

| happy | sad | afraid | bored |

6. The grasshopper feels _____ when the story ends.

| happy | sad | afraid | bored |

Side 1

Side 2

| ful | less |

1. hopeless _____
2. painful _____
3. restless _____
4. careful _____

5. fearful _____
6. powerless _____
7. joyful _____
8. harmless _____

Side 3

Name _____

January, February, March → **January**
February

April, May, June → April

| un | less | ful |

1. healthy _____   6. restful _____

2. lucky _____   7. unlock _____

3. careless _____   8. harmless _____

4. hopeful _____   9. unfold _____

5. clear _____

1. is sams bike fast or slow

2. a cat a dog and a bird are in anas yard

3. pablo and i will go to bills house

4. did you see snakes lions and apes at the zoo

True	False

1. Ice is cold. _____

2. Cats have ears. _____

3. Fish climb trees. _____

Name _____

January, February, March → **January**
February
_____

April, May, June → April
_____

| ful | un | less |

1. hopeless _____

2. lock _____

3. fold _____

4. harmless _____

5. careful _____

6. painful _____

7. fair _____

Side 1

| short | pull | clean | push | tall | dirty |

1. I am going to push the wagon.

2. My hands are dirty.

3. She is as short as her sister.

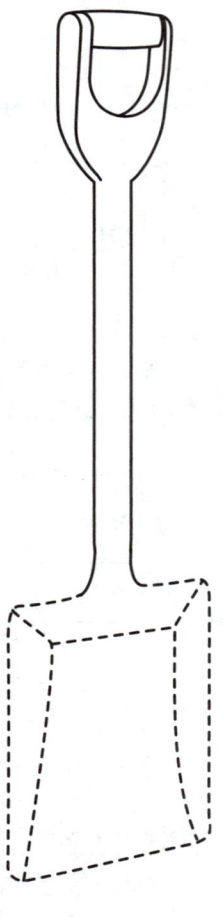

Side 2

Name _____

January, February, March →   January

April, May, June →

| shout | cry | full | well | over |

1. above _____   3. healthy _____

2. weep _____   4. yell _____

1. tom rita and i rode bikes to the lake

2. do you see marias sister here

3. we need to buy books and paper

4. can robs dog come to the park

---

animals	food	buildings

Side 2

Name _____

over   shut   cry   close   above   weep

1. Ask Jim to shut the window.

2. Hold your hands over your head.

3. My little brother will weep.

The plane will fly.

The baby

Name _____

46

Side 1

January, February, March →

January

April, May, June →

| under | small | large | little | big | below |

1. The cat is very small.

2. Is the ball under the table?

3. A big dog barked.

Side 2

Name _____

47

containers   furniture   clothing

Side 1

on   chair

The cat was sitting in the grass.
The dog

Name _____

48

True   False

1. A book is made of paper. _____

2. Ice cream is cold. _____

3. A bed is furniture. _____

Side 1

table

The dog was sitting on the floor.
The cat

winter   spring   summer   fall

Name _____

| weep | healthy | yell | cry | shout | well |

1. The boy's dog was healthy.

2. Sam's baby will cry.

3. That cop had to yell.

Side 1

	True	False

1. A bottle is a plant. _____

2. Lamps give light. _____

3. The moon grows in the ground. _____

---

vehicles	containers	tools

Name

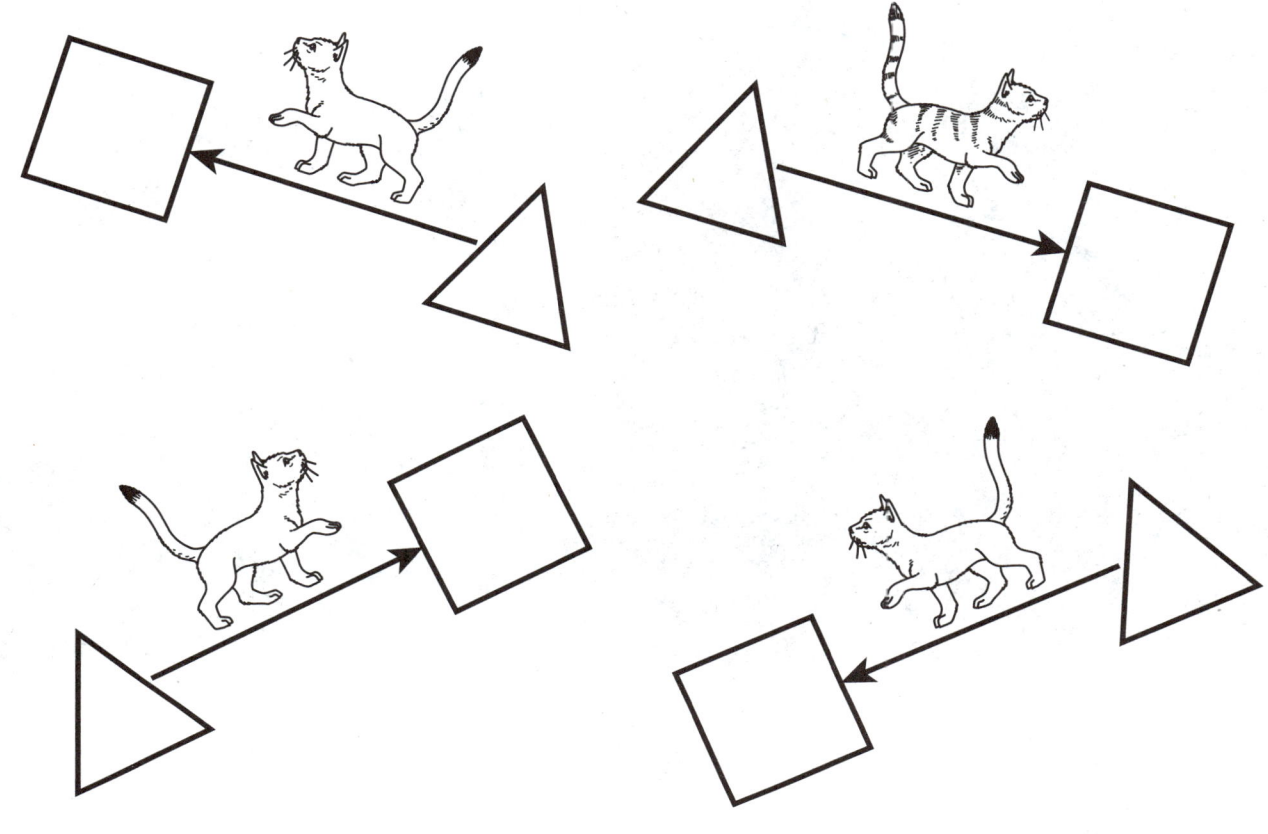

January, February, March ⟶

April, May, June ⟶

Side 1

horse

The boy was riding a bike.
The girl

Side 3

Name _____

| True | False |

1. Cold air is lighter than hot air. _____

2. Hot air makes balloons rise in the sky. _____

3. People made kites out of metal and glass. _____

4. Bamboo is a kind of cloth. _____

5. Silk is very heavy. _____

6. A festival is a big party. _____

7. People used lanterns to send messages. _____

8. Balloons carry people in baskets. _____

 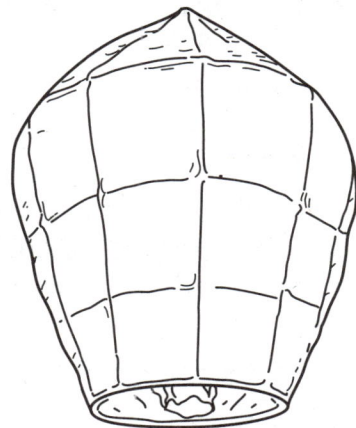

Side 1

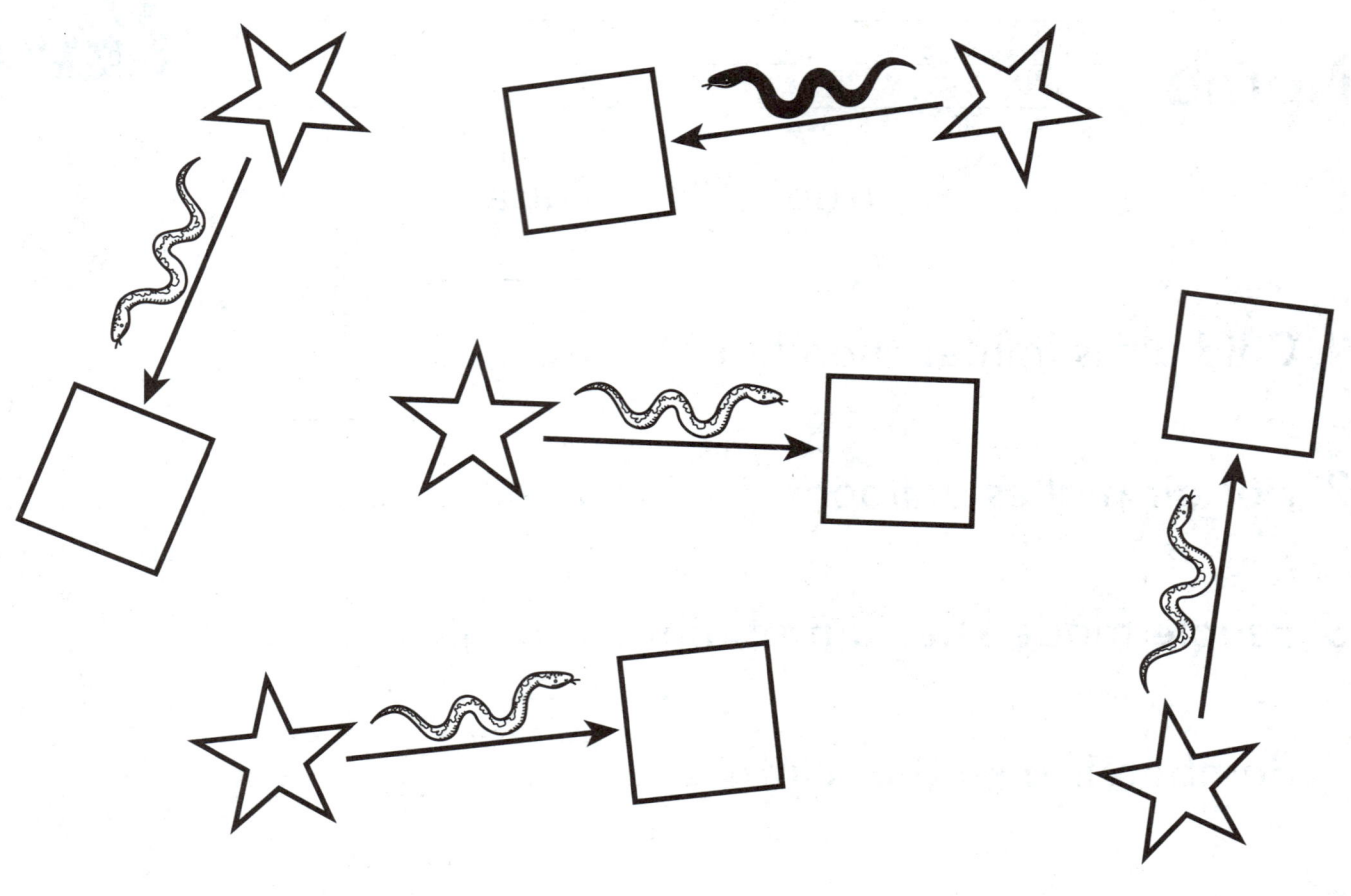

| slow | tall | short | hard | fast | easy |

1. The test was easy for Sam's sister.

2. I saw a very tall building.

3. I like to ride in fast boats.

Side 2

Name _____

52

January, February, March →

April, May, June →

July, August, September →

September

| True | False |

1. People eat vehicles. _____

2. A table is furniture. _____

3. A saw is made of paper. _____

Side 1

bike

The girl rode an elephant.
The boy

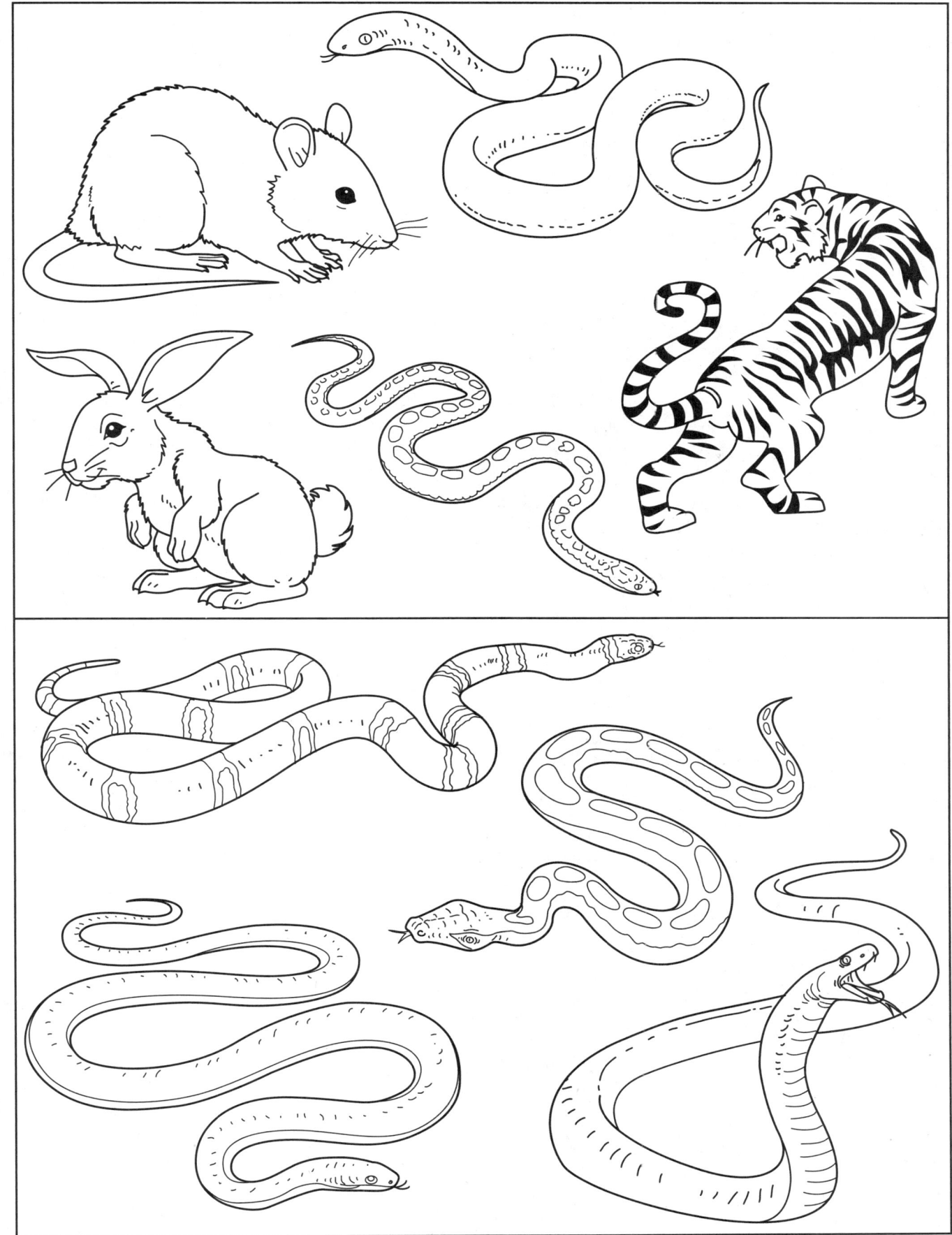

Side 3

Name _____

January, February, March →

April, May, June →

July, August, September →

September

| True | False |

1. You wear shoes on your head. _____

2. A box is a building. _____

3. An airplane goes in the air. _____

Side 1

fast   under   little   below   quick   small

1. A small boy ran in the park.

2. The cat hid under my bed.

3. I want to ride a fast bike.

Side 2

Name

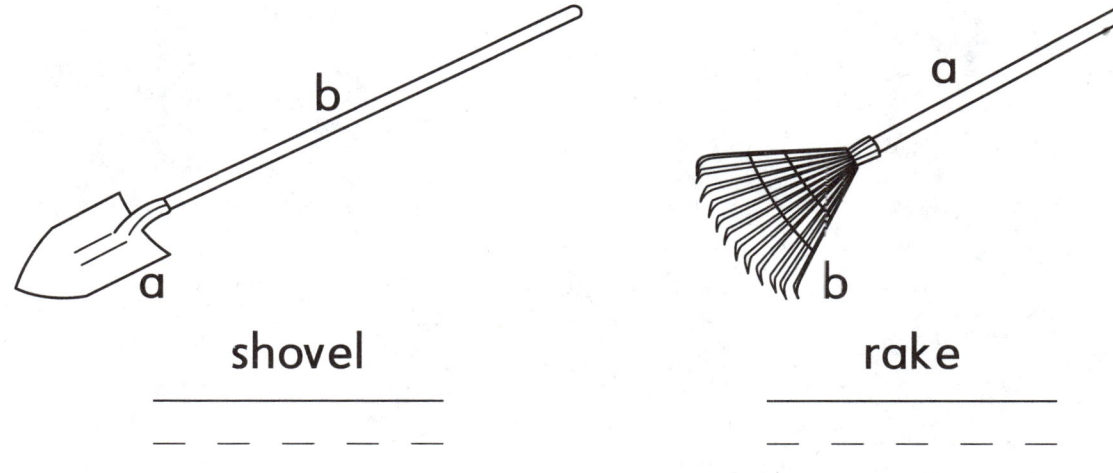

shovel

rake

Sunday   Monday   Tuesday   Wednesday
Thursday   Friday   Saturday

Side 1

girl   book

The boy read a paper.

Side 2

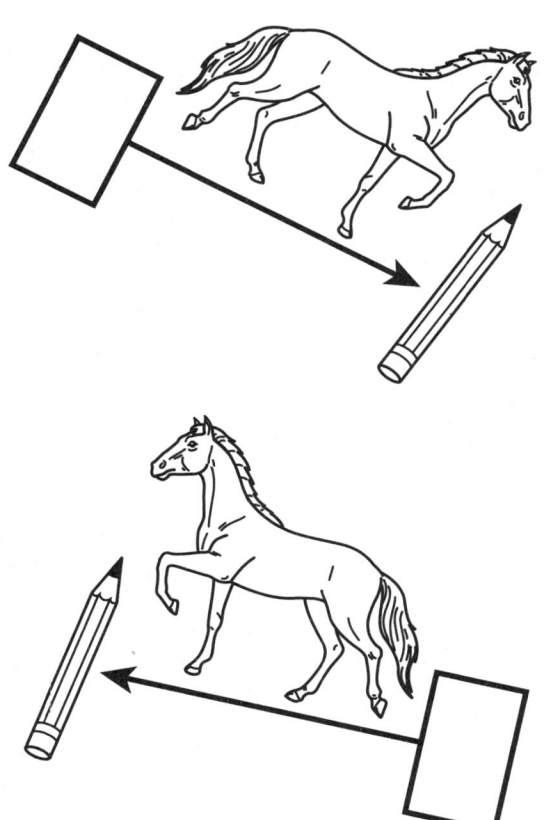
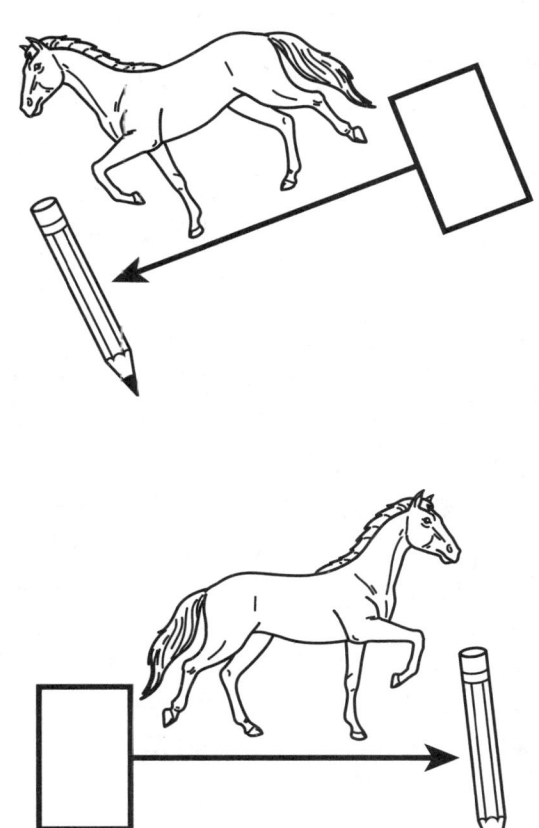

Side 3

Name _____

55

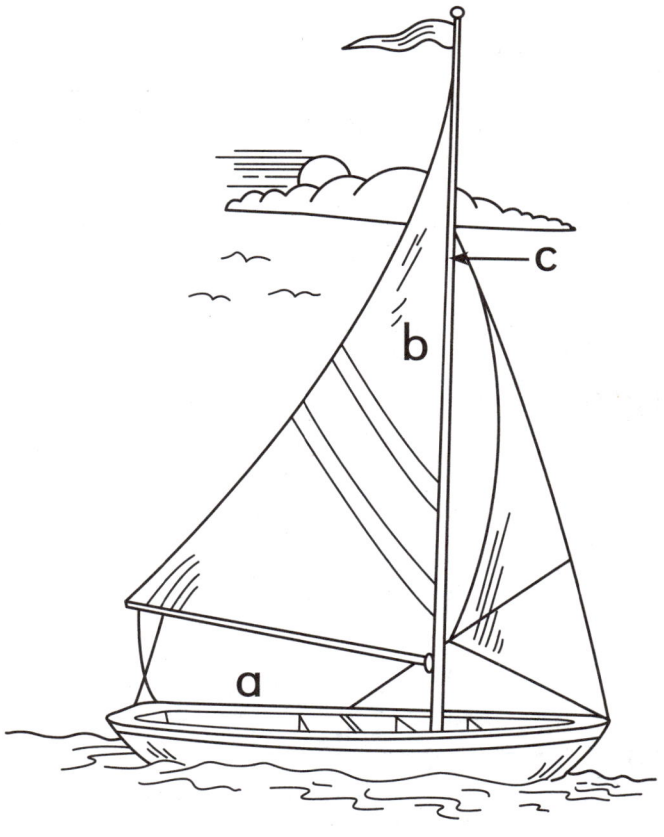

sailboat

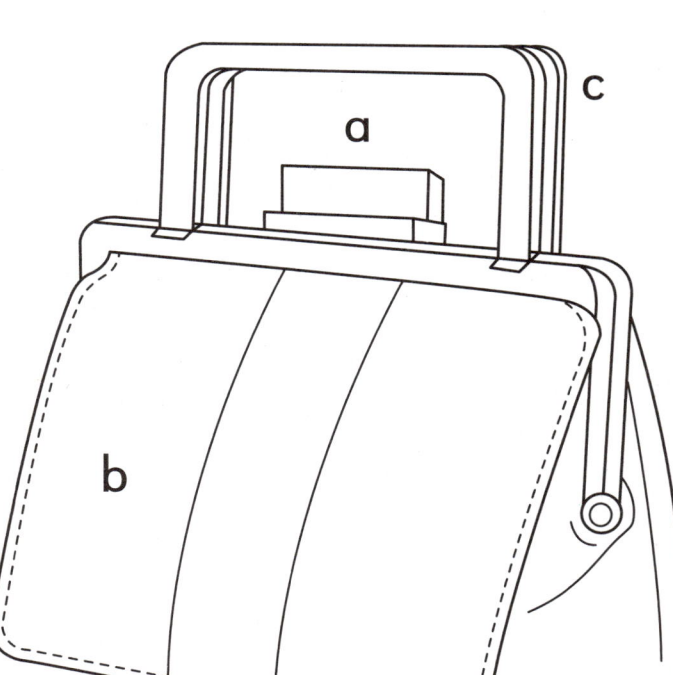

purse

Side 1

January, February, March →

April, May, June →

July, August, September →

Side 2

| little | narrow | noisy | quiet | big | wide |

1. A big dog barked at the car.

2. It is noisy in the classroom.

3. That house has a wide door.

Side 3

Name _____

56

1. _____ fell into a stream.

2. _____ chased mice in a castle.

3. _____ sat in the sun on a log.

4. _____ worked hard in the summer.

5. _____ carried water in a bucket.

6. _____ had no food when the winter came.

7. _____ tricked a shark to help some fish.

Side 1

	True	False

1. Chickens give milk. _____

2. You eat clothing. _____

3. You can ride on a horse. _____

boy   floor

The girl was standing on a chair.

Side 3

Name _____

57

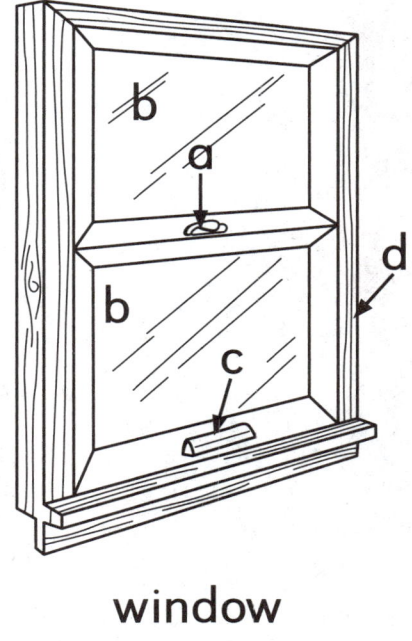

window

Side 1

dog   floor

A cat was sleeping on the chair.
A dog

January, February, March ⟶

April, May, June ⟶

July, August, September ⟶

Side 3

Name _____

58

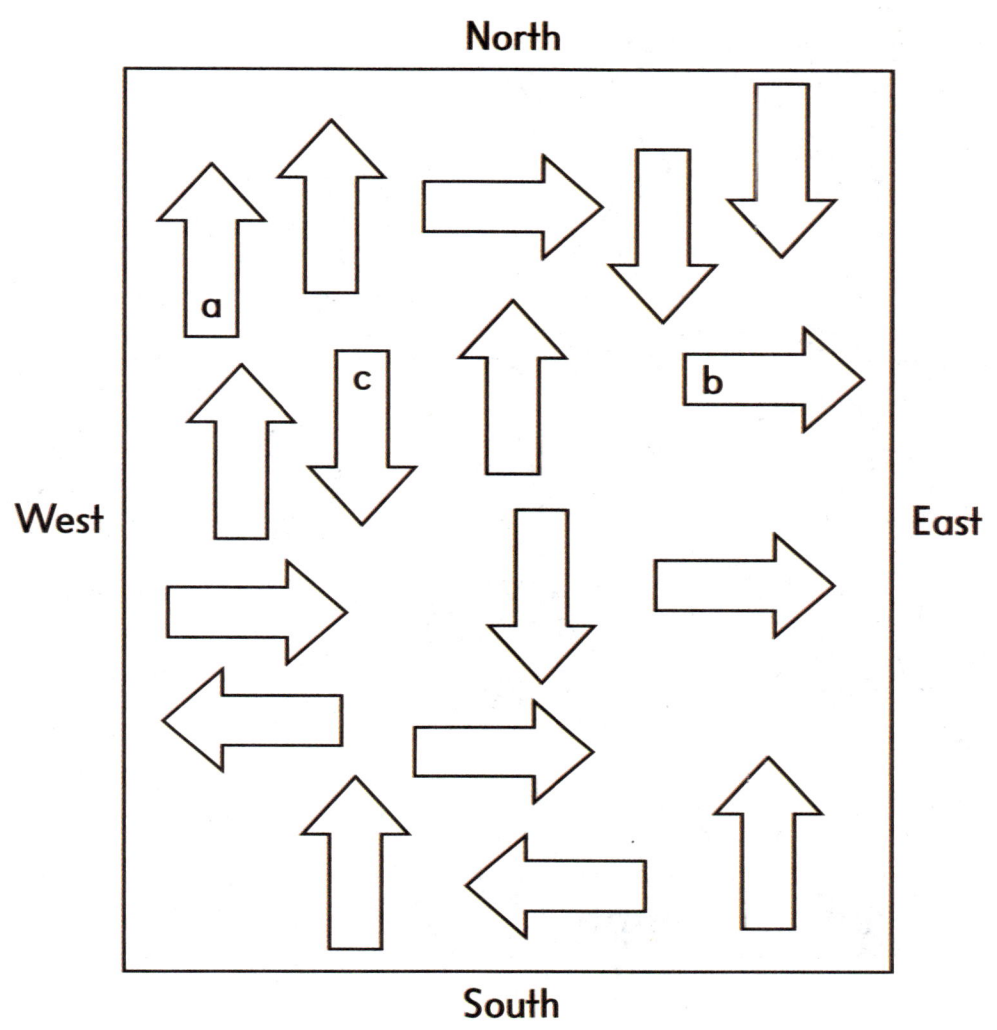

| True | False |

1. Farm animals live in barns. _____

2. People have feathers. _____

3. You find the moon in the sky. _____

Side 1

fast   old   empty   slow   full   young

1. The young woman swam in the pool.

2. Tom's cabinet was empty.

3. Can that car drive fast?

Name

59

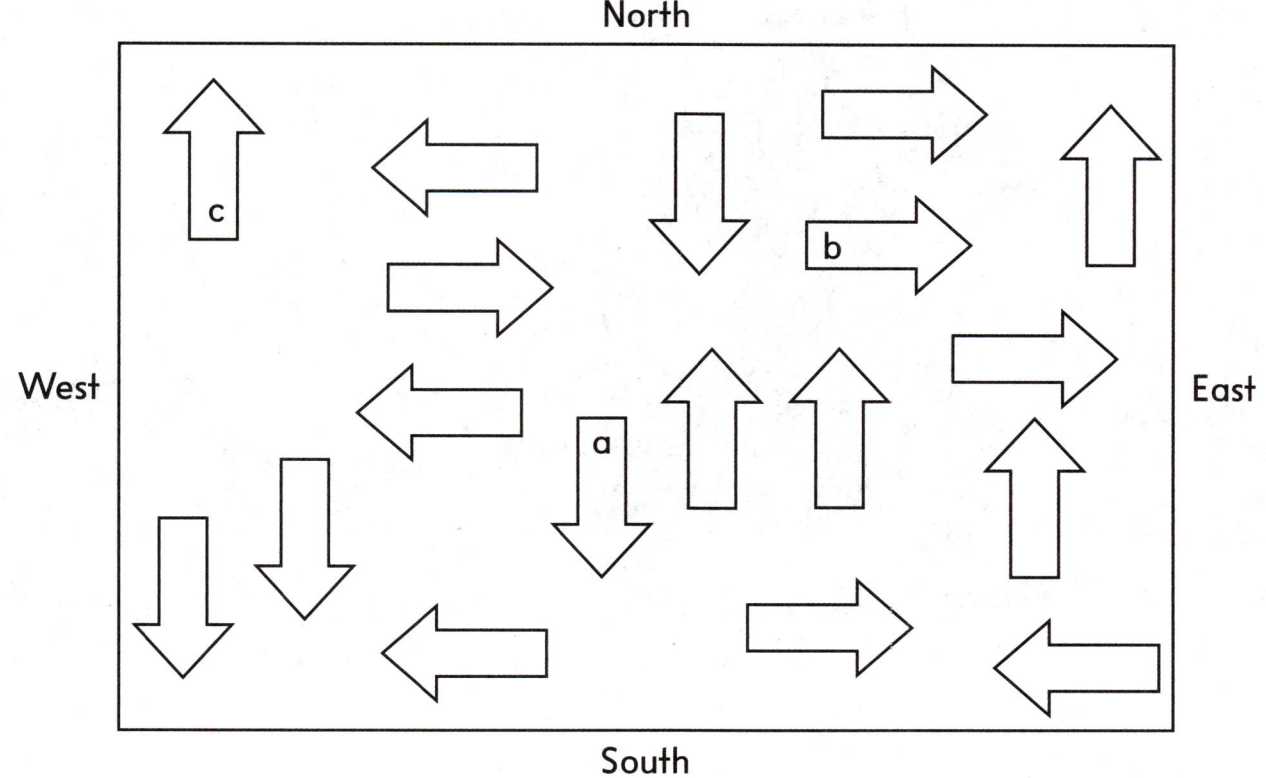

Side 1

pail

The man had mail.
The cat

January, February, March →

April, May, June →

July, August, September →

Name _____

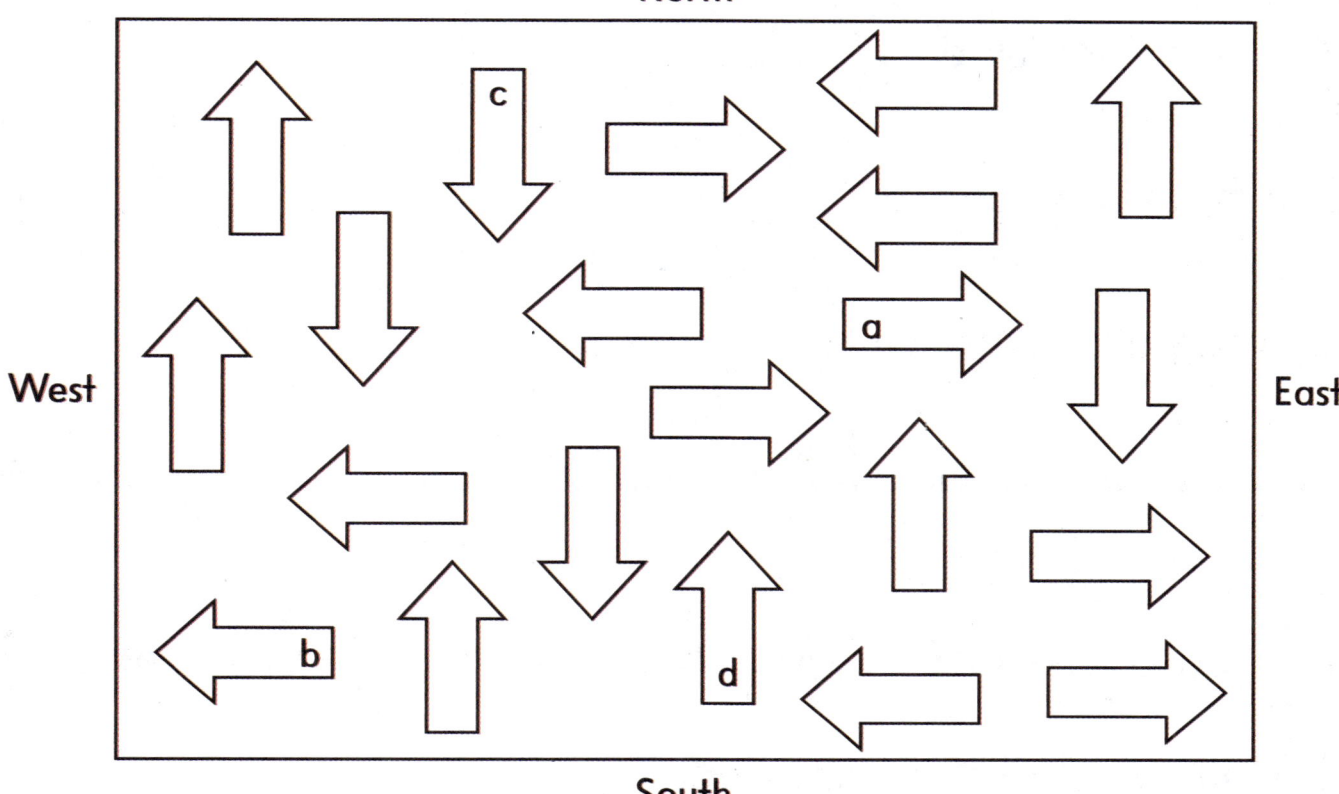

| winter | spring | summer | fall |

Side 1

	True	False

1. A boat has wheels. _____

2. A boat has roots. _____

3. A table is furniture. _____

| shut | skinny | healthy | close | thin | well |

1. Will you shut the front door?
   _____
   _____

2. All the kittens are healthy.
   _____
   _____

3. The giraffe had a thin neck.
   _____
   _____

Name _____

61

Side 1

| dairy | climate | crops | cotton | pests |

1. Farmers grow _____ in fields.

2. Milk and cheese are _____ foods.

3. Facts about _____ tell how much rain will fall.

4. Most clothes are made of _____ .

5. _____ are insects that destroy plants.

Side 2

Name _____

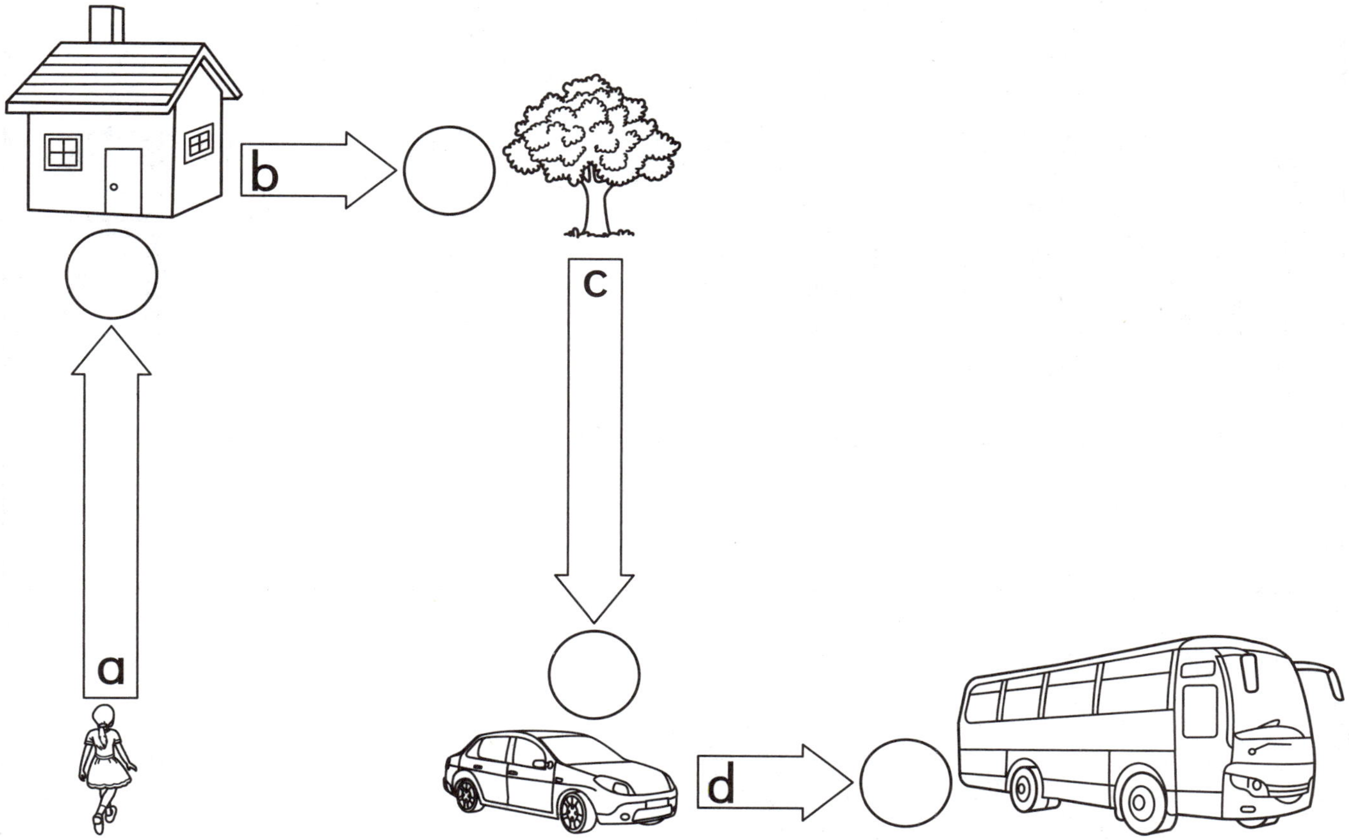

62

Side 1

Side 2

book   boy   reading

The girl was drawing a picture.

Side 3

Name _____

63

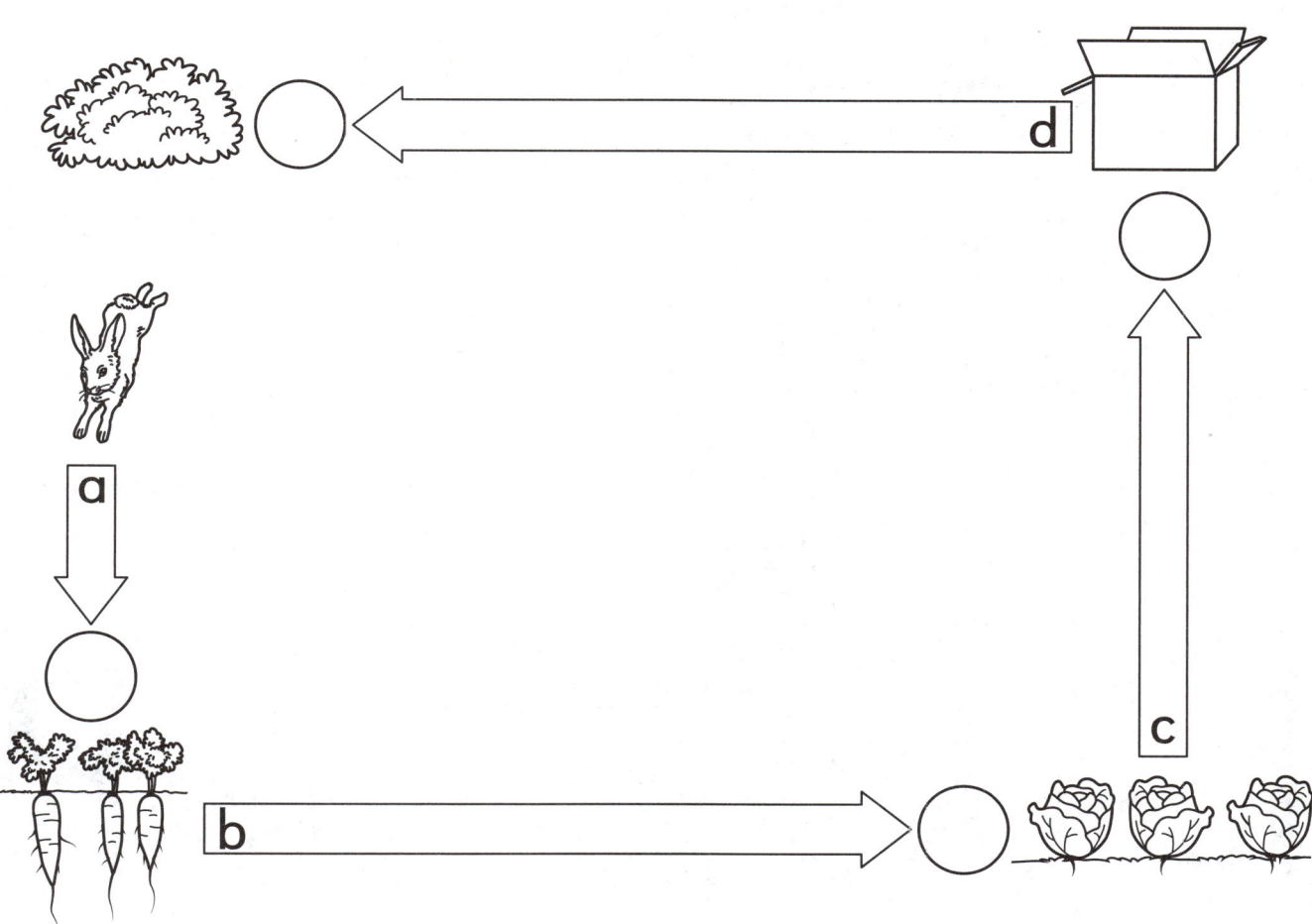

Side 1

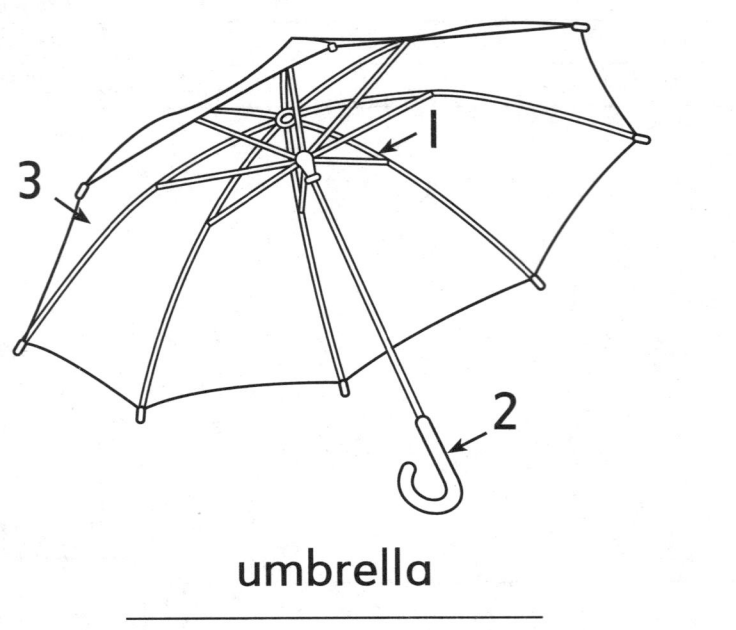

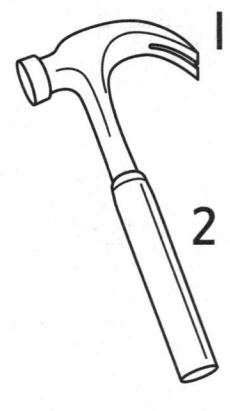

umbrella

hammer

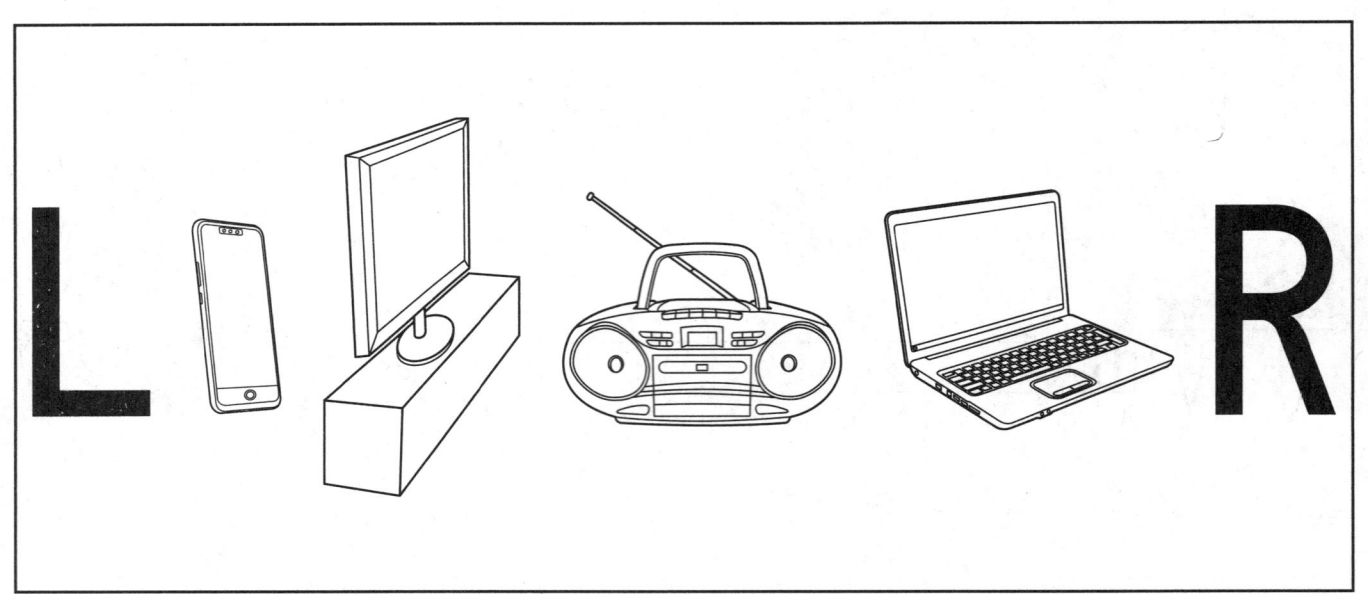

Side 2

January, February, March →

April, May, June →

July, August, September →

October, November, December →

Side 3

Name

64

Side 1

January, February, March →

April, May, June →

July, August, September →

October, November, December →

Side 2

milk　　poured　　some　　banana　　peeled

The boy

The girl

Side 3

Name _____

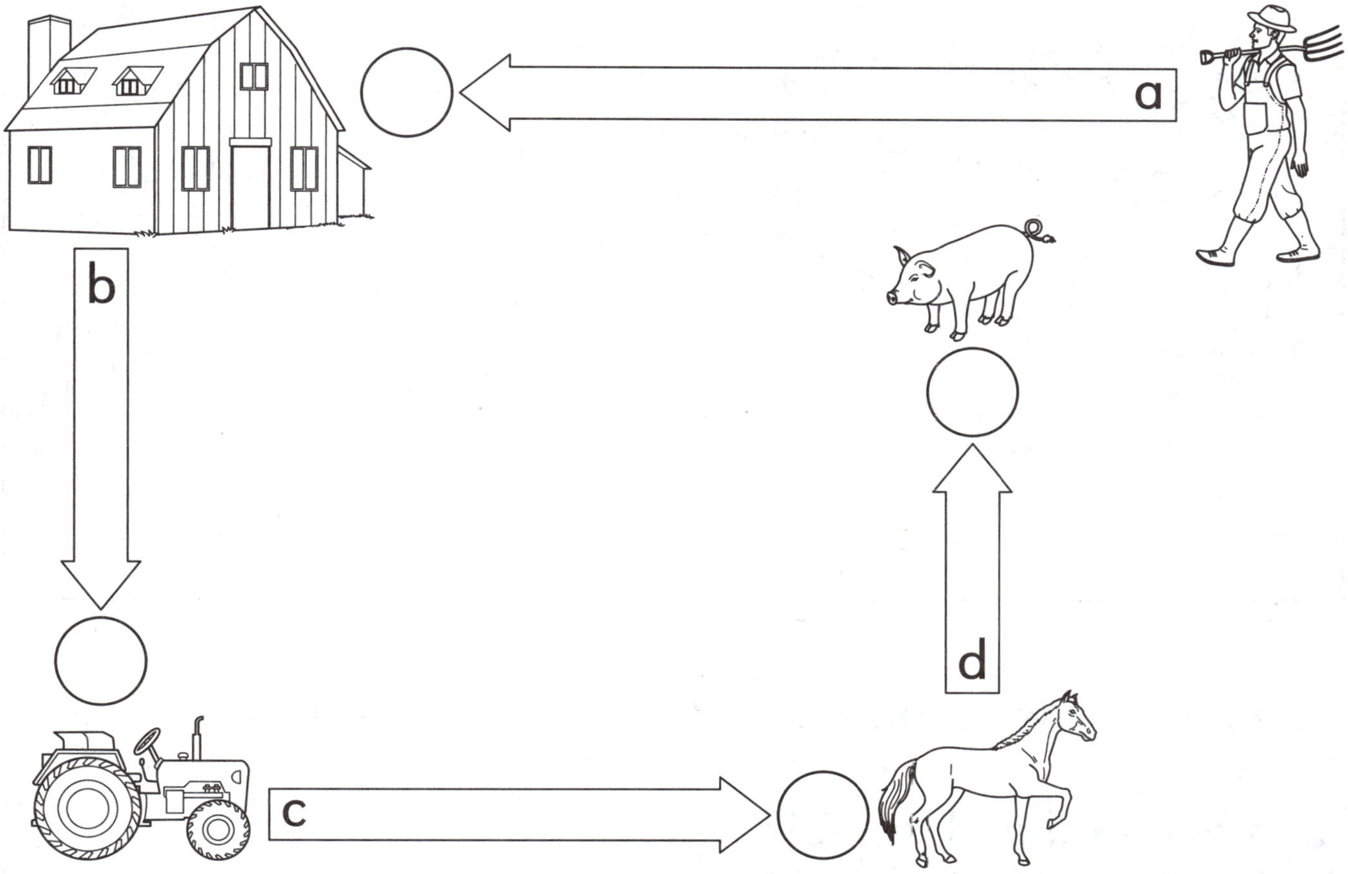

65

Side 1

wide　　raw　　pulled　　cooked　　narrow　　pushed

1. Is the food on the table raw?

2. My mom's brother pushed the car on Thursday.

3. That barn has wide doors.

Side 2

Name

66

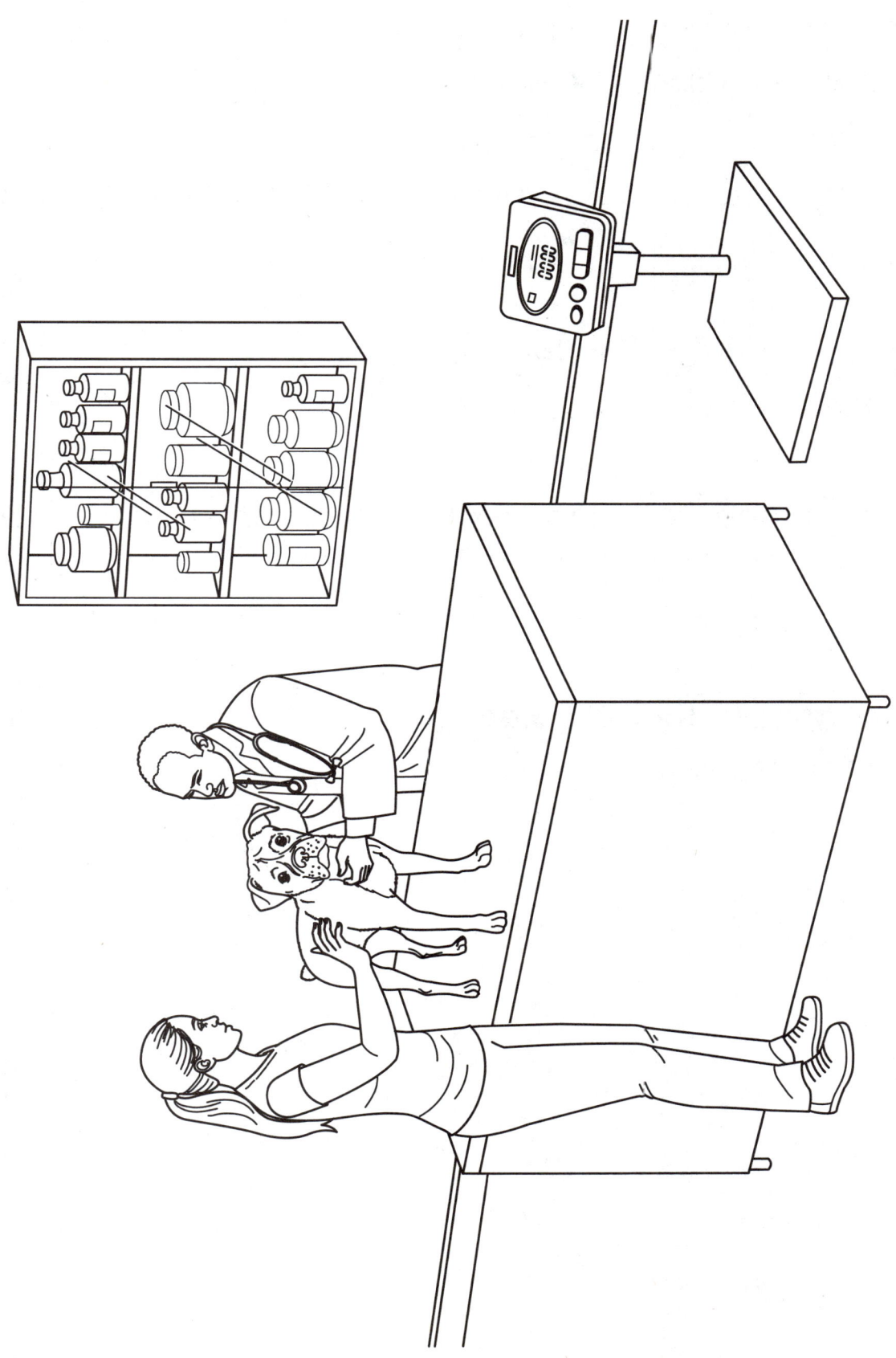

Side 1

| surgery | diet | specialist | disease | clinic |

1. Most veterinarians work in a _____ .

2. A _____ works on a farm, at a zoo, or at a park.

3. A dog with a broken leg may need _____ to get well.

4. Healthy food and clean water are parts of an animal's _____ .

5. Veterinarians look for signs of _____ during a checkup.

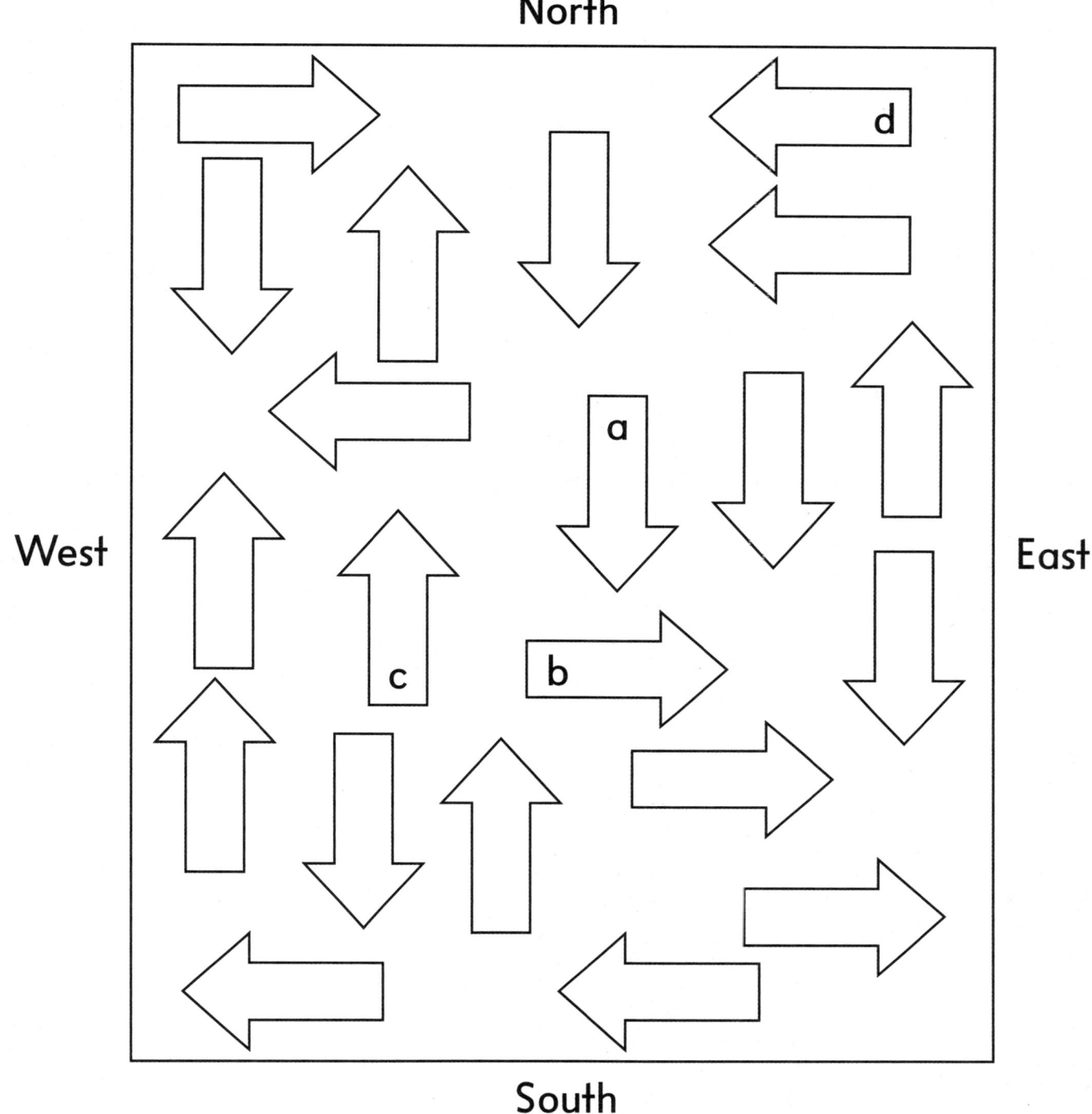

Name _____

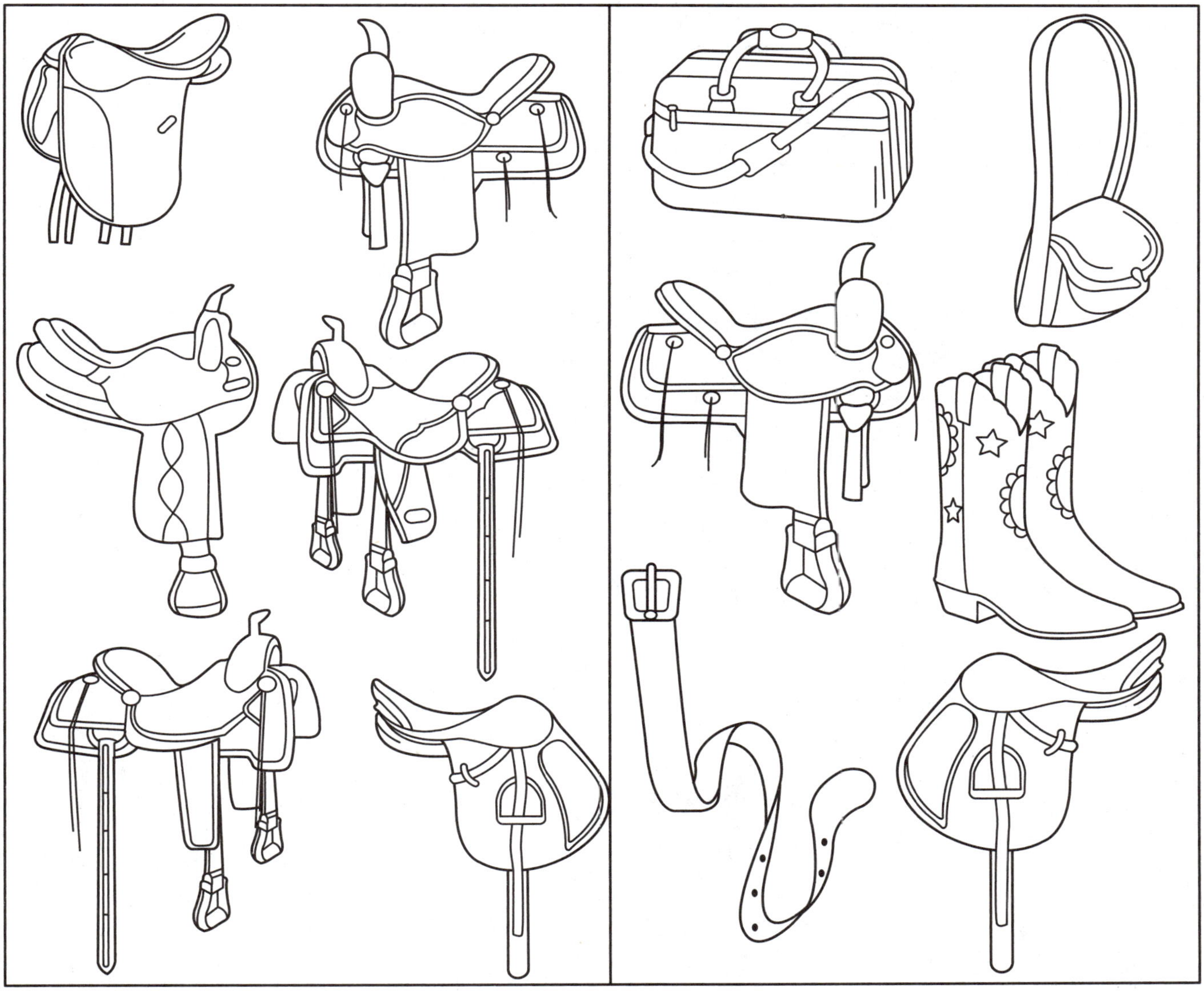

67

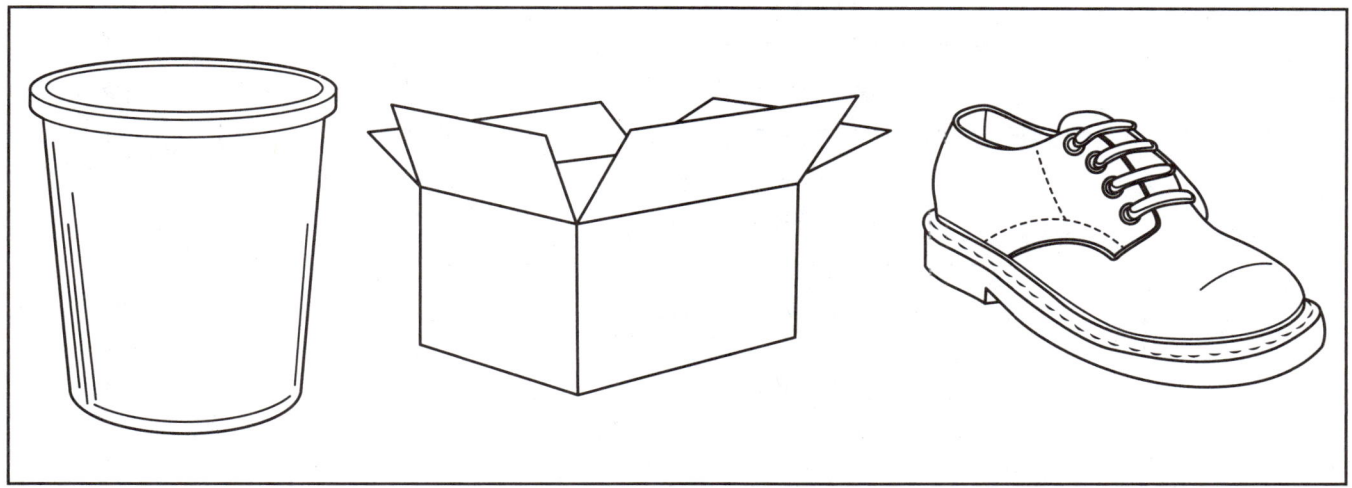

Side 1

Sunday	Monday	Tuesday	Wednesday
Thursday	Friday	Saturday

| an apple | an orange | peeled | ate |

The girl

The boy

Side 3

Name _____

68

hard   shiny   alike   bright   difficult   easy

1. I will take a hard test on Monday.

2. Sam's dog wore a shiny collar.

3. Is the color of these toys the same?

Side 1

Side 2

January, February, March →

April, May, June →

July, August, September →

October, November, December →

Name _____

| True | False |

1. A boat has wheels. _____

2. A boat has roots. _____

3. A table is furniture. _____

Side 1

| cloth | metal | glass |

standing　　　sitting　　　table　　　wagon

The dog

The cat

Name _____

1. A _____ takes care of animals.   farmer   veterinarian

2. A _____ protects the land.   farmer   veterinarian

3. A _____ works in a clinic.   farmer   veterinarian

4. A _____ uses tools to do work.   farmer   veterinarian

5. A _____ knows a lot about the climate.   farmer   veterinarian

6. A _____ grows crops.   farmer   veterinarian

7. A _____ can do surgery.   farmer   veterinarian

8. A _____ studies diseases.   farmer   veterinarian

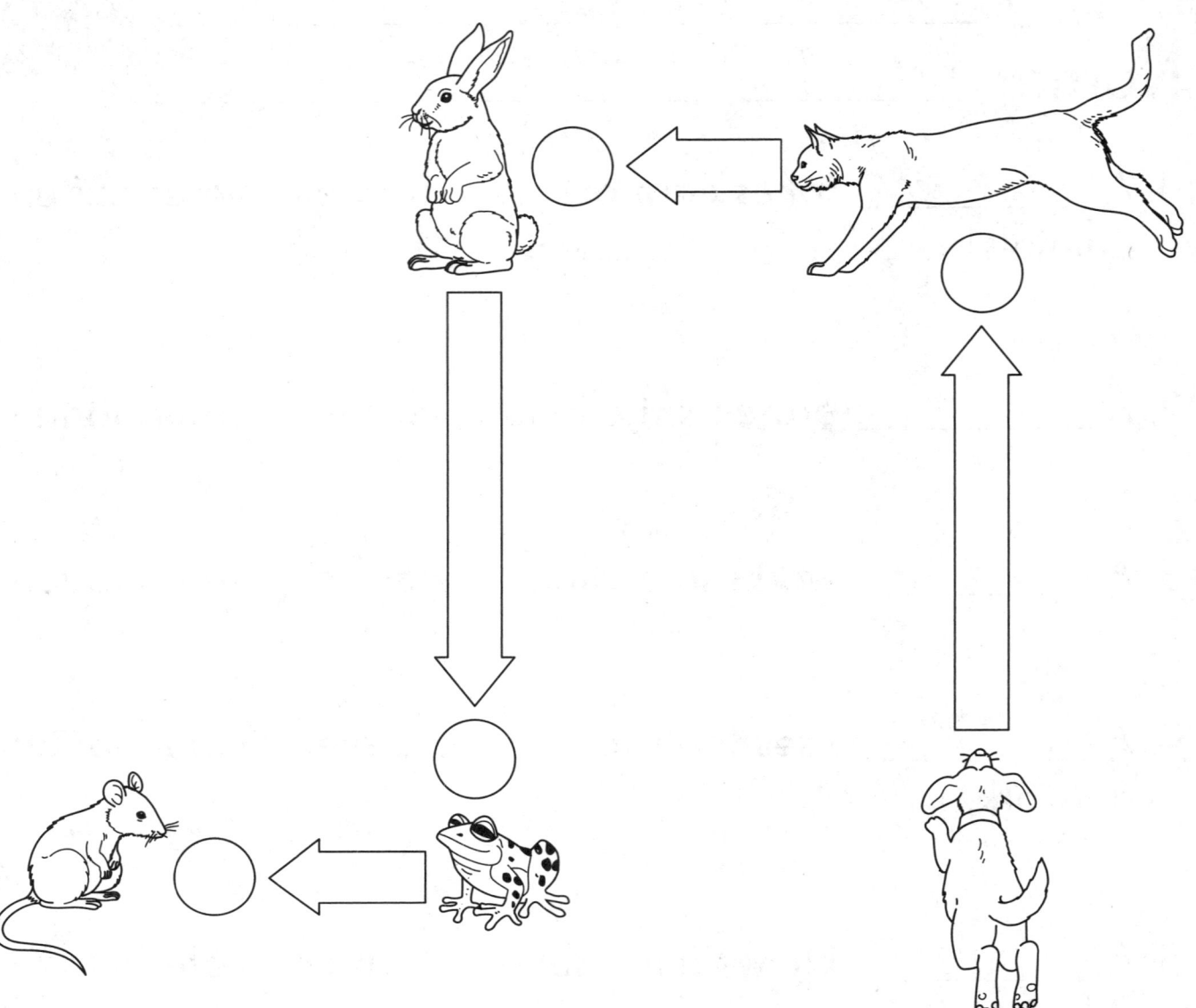

Side 2

January, February, March →

April, May, June →

July, August, September →

October, November, December →

Name _____

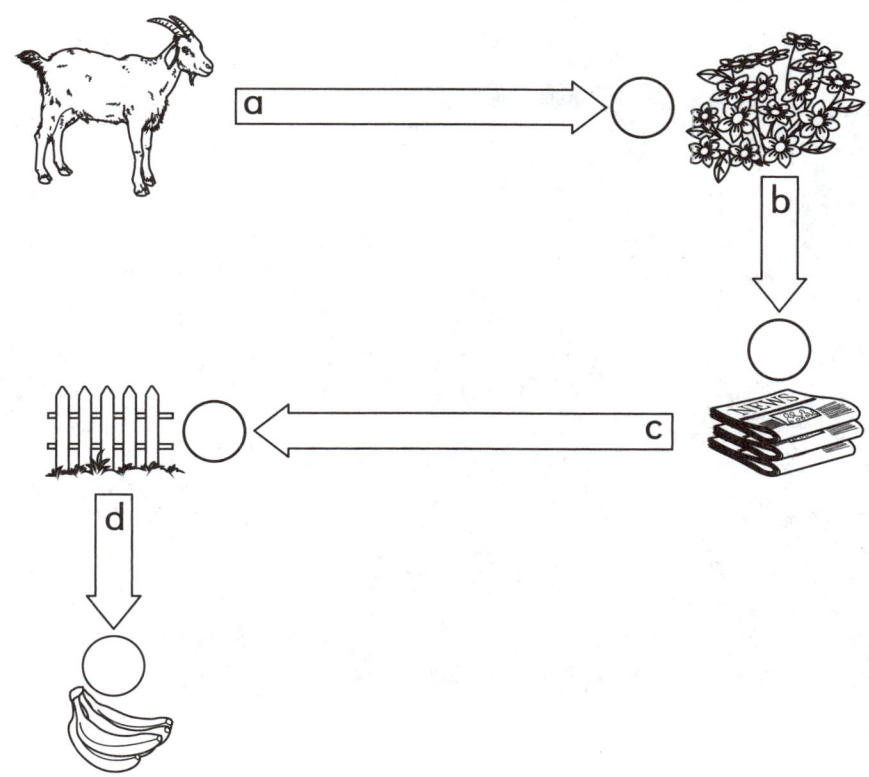

Side 1

apple   gave   horse   some   medicine

The farmer
The vet

Name _____

January, February, March →

April, May, June →

July, August, September →

October, November, December →

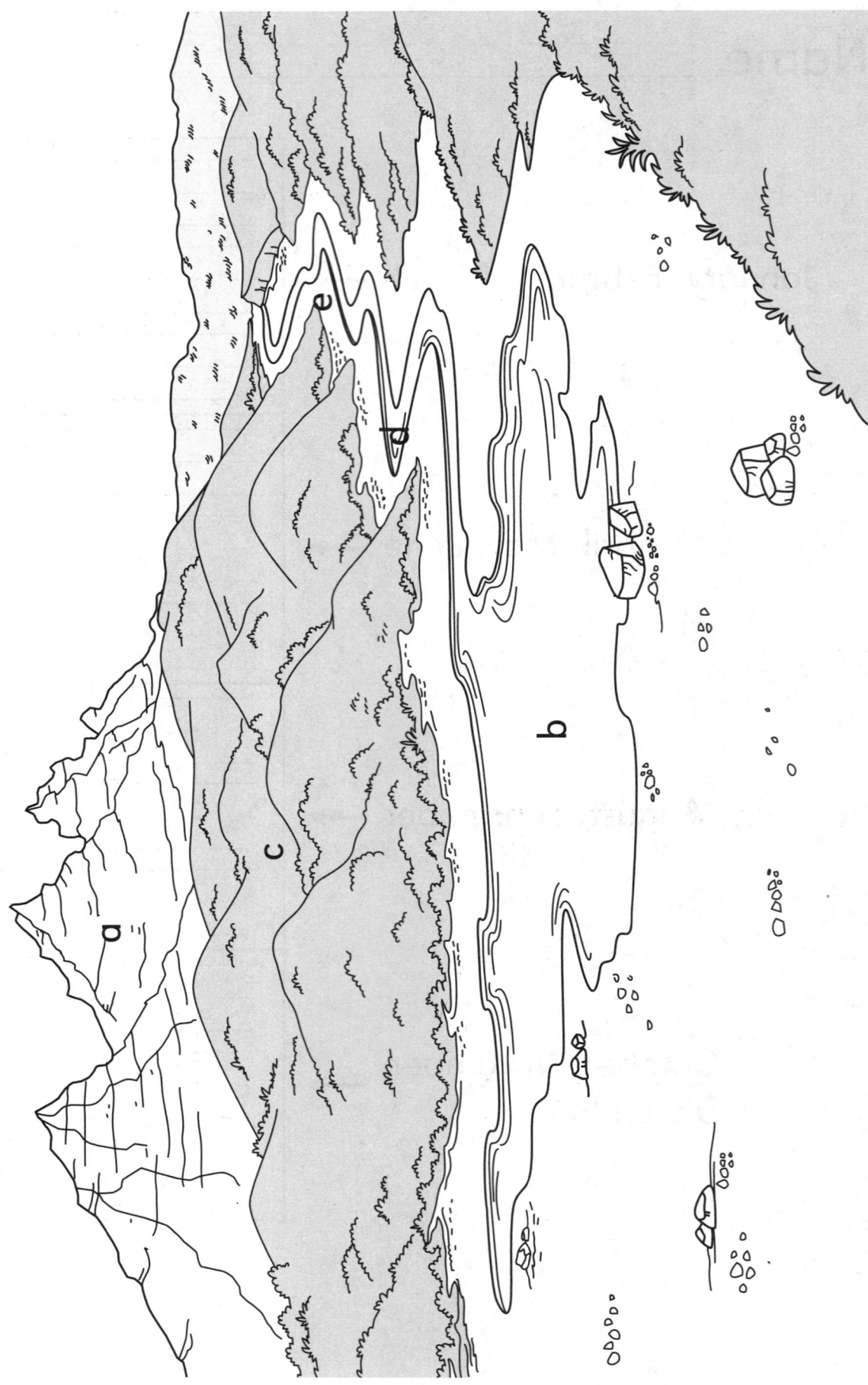

Side 2

| short | big | tail | sail |

The cat
The boat

Name _____

73

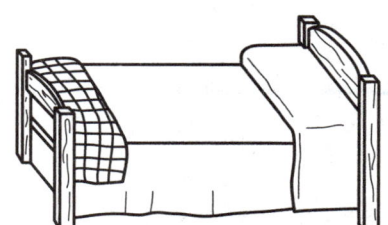

Side 1

deep   rough   shallow   safe   smooth   dangerous

1. The lake was very deep.

2. Does this paper feel rough?

3. Sam's cat ran down a dangerous path.

Name _____

74

 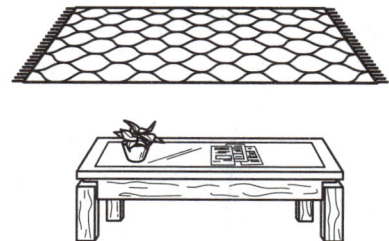 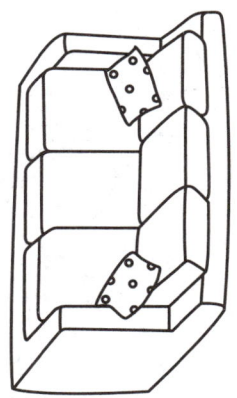

| winter | spring | summer | fall |

Side 1

end　　near　　finish　　over　　close to　　above

1. The race will finish soon.

2. Are we near downtown yet?

3. Planes fly over the city at night.

Side 2

Name _____ 75

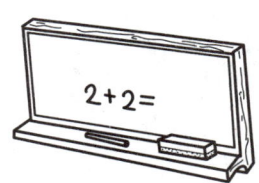

| True | False |

1. You use a fork when you eat. _____

2. People live in restaurants. _____

3. A box is a building. _____

Side 1

January, February, March →

April, May, June →

July, August, September →

October, November, December →

Side 2

PHOTO CREDITS

L001 Side 01 (tl)lynx/iconotec.com/Glow Images, (tc)Yanas/Shutterstock, (tr)Judith Collins/Alamy, (cl)Clover/SuperStock, (cl)©Mark Dierker/McGraw-Hill Education, (c)PhotoDisc, (c)Author's Image/Glow Images, (cr)Kim DeClaire/iStock/Getty Images, (cr)Stockbyte/Getty Images, (bc)C Squared Studios/Getty Images, (br)Brand X Pictures/Stockbyte/Getty Images, (br)McGraw-Hill Education; **L004 Side 01** (tl)Andrey_Kuzmin/iStock/Getty Images, (tc)McGraw-Hill Education, (tr)CORBIS, (bl)Mark Steinmetz/McGraw-Hill Education, (bc)Ingram Publishing/SuperStock, (br)Nicholas Eveleigh/Digital Vision/Getty Images; **L006 Side 01** (tl)Henrik5000/Getty Images, (tcl)Darryl Brooks/Shutterstock.com, (tcr)©Jules Frazier/Getty Images, (tcr)NASA Langley/Advanced Concepts Lab, AMA, Inc., (tr)Clover/SuperStock, (cl)aguirre_mar/iStock/Getty Images, (cr)©Author's Image/Glow Images, (bl)Ingram Publishing/Alamy, (bl)Lauren Burke/Photographer's Choice RF/Getty Images, (bc)nattanan726/Shutterstock.com, (br)Alexey Seafarer/Shutterstock; **L006 Side 02** (tl)Andrey_Kuzmin/iStock/Getty Images, (tcl)Author's Image/Glow Images, (tcr)McGraw-Hill Education, (tr)CORBIS, (cl)McGraw-Hill Education, (c)ronniechua/123RF, (bc)CORBIS, (br)Andrey_Kuzmin/iStock/Getty Images; **L007 Side 01** (tl)Ingram Publishing/SuperStock, (tcl)McGraw-Hill Education, (tcr)©Purestock/SuperStock, (tr)©Ingram Publishing/SuperStock, (cl)C Squared Studios/Photodisc/Getty Images, (cl)Artbox/Shutterstock.com, (cr)Stockbyte/PunchStock, (cr)Anton Starikov/Alamy Stock Photo, (bl)aguirre_mar/iStock/Getty Images, (bc)Georgii Dolgykh/123RF, (br)U.S. Air Force photo by Lisa M. Macias; **L007 Side 02** (tl)Lauren Burke/Photographer's Choice RF/Getty Images, (tcl)Eyebyte/Alamy, (tcr)McGraw-Hill Education, (tr)Kim DeClaire/iStock/Getty Images, (cl)Kim DeClaire/iStock/Getty Images, (cl)McGraw-Hill Education, (cr)Eyebyte/Alamy, (cr)Lauren Burke/Photographer's Choice RF/Getty Images, (bl)Ingram Publishing/SuperStock, (bcl)Lauren Burke/Photographer's Choice RF/Getty Images, (bcr)Malosee Dolo/123RF, (br)McGraw-Hill Education; **L008 Side 01** (tl)McGraw-Hill Education, (tcl)lynx/iconotec.com/Glow Images, (tcr)McGraw-Hill Education, (tr)lynx/iconotec.com/Glow Images, (bl)Stockbyte/Getty Images, (bcl)Spaces Images/Blend Images, (bcr)Martin Ruegner/Getty Images, (br)pinstock/Getty Images; **L008 Side 02** (tl)Hutchings Photography/Digital Light Source, (tcr)lynx/iconotec.com/Glow Images, (tr)Ken Karp/McGraw-Hill Education, (cl)lynx/iconotec.com/Glow Images, (c)G.K. & Vikki Hart/Getty Images, (bl)Jupiter Images, (bc)Ken Karp/McGraw-Hill Education, (br)Hutchings Photography/Digital Light Source; **L010 Side 02** (tl)Dot Box Inc./McGraw-Hill Education, (tc)Iconotec/Glow Images, (tr)Dimitris66/E+/Getty Images, (cl)Iconotec/Glow Images, (c)ronniechua/123RF, (cr)Dot Box Inc./McGraw-Hill Education, (bl)pbakerp/iStock/Getty Images, (bc)Dimitris66/E+/Getty Images; **L011 Side 01** (tl)hsvrs/iStock/Getty Images, (tr)Alexander Dunkel/E+/Getty Images, (bl)Stockbyte/Getty Images, (br)Siede Preis/Getty Images; **L012 Side 01** (tl)supertrooper123RF.com, (tr)maxpayne222123RF.com, (bl)©Photodisc/Getty Images, (br)Andriy Popov/123RF.com; **L013 Side 01** (tl)yevgeniy11/Shutterstock.com, (tr)Juniors Bildarchiv/Alamy, (cl)Mark Steinmetz, (cr)Photo by Robert Colletta,USDA-ARS, (bl)McGraw-Hill Education, (br)Iconotec/Glow Images; **L017 Side 01** (tl)David Planchet, (tr)maykal/123RF, (cl)©Perfect Picture Parts/Alamy, (cl)CORBIS, (cr)pinstock/Getty Images, (cr)Ryan McVay/Getty Images, (bl)Stockbyte/Getty Images, (br)Shutterstock/Lucky-photographer; **L019 Side 01** (tl)wabeno/iStock/Getty Images, (tr)Oleksiy Maksymenko/Alamy, (cl)Ingram Publishing/SuperStock, (cr)McGraw-Hill Education, (bl)Stockbyte/PunchStock, (br)Alex Cao/Digital Vision/Getty Images; **L024 Side 01** (tl)Cleveland Metroparks Zoo/McGraw-Hill Education, (tcl)Comstock Images/Alamy, (tcr)C Squared Studios/Getty Images, (tr)gladassfanny/Getty Images, (bl)NASA Langley/Advanced Concepts Lab, AMA, Inc., (bcl)©Wojtek Kalinowski Photography/CORBIS, (bcr)©imAgeBroker/Superstock, (br)Ingram Publishing/SuperStock; **L028 Side 01** (cl)tonobalaguer 123RF.com, (c)Comstock Images/Alamy Stock Photo, (cr)aguirre_mar/iStock/Getty Images, (r)scanrail 123RF.com, **L029 Side 01** (l)Ingram Publishing/SuperStock, (cl)anastasia tsoupa/123RF.com, (cr)Lorcan/Digital Vision/Getty Images, (r)Ken Karp/McGraw-Hill Education; **L029 Side 02** (tl)ami mataraj/Shutterstock.com, (tr)Timolina/Shutterstock, (cl)atoss/123RF, (cr)C Squared Studios/Getty Images, (bl)McGraw-Hill Education, (br)Siede Preis/Getty Images; **L030 Side 01** (cl)Shutterstock/vipman, (l)Jan Tadeusz/Alamy Images, (cr)Andrey_Kuzmin/iStock/Getty Images, (r)D. Hurst/Alamy; **L031 Side 02** (l)Evgeny Karandaev/Shutterstock.com, (cl)McGraw-Hill Education, (cr)Mark Steinmetz, (r)Jeffrey Coolidge/Getty Images; **L033 Side 02** (cl)Mark Steinmetz/McGraw-Hill Education, (l)Comstock Images/Alamy, (cr)C Squared Studios/Getty Images, (r)lynx/iconotec.com/Glow Images; **L037 Side 01** (cl)Comstock/Stockbyte/Getty Images, (tr)Lars A. Niki, (cr)Martin Ruegner/Getty Images, (cl)anastasia tsoupa/123RF.com, (cl)lynx/iconotec.com/Glow Images, (cr)Ingram Publishing/SuperStock, (cr)Spaces Images/Blend Images, (cr)Stockbyte/Getty Images, (bl)Artbox/Shutterstock.com, (br)C Squared Studios/Getty Images; **L038 Side 01** (t)Creative Crop/Digital Vision/Getty Images, (tc)Denise McCullough, (c)RTimages/Alamy, (b)McGraw-Hill Education, (bc)Sharon Montrose/Getty Images; **L039 Side 01** (t)vitalytyagunov/123RF, (c)McGraw-Hill Education, (c)Jules Frazier/Getty Images, (b)Katarzyna Bialasiewicz/123RF; **L040 Side 01** (t)Peter Turner/Shutterstock.com, (c)Khongkit Wiriyachan/123RF, (c pzAxe/Shutterstock, (b)McGraw-Hill Education; **L040 Side 02** (t)McGraw-Hill Education. Mark Dierker, photographer, (tr)ronniechua/123RF, (cl)Songphon Kotesopha/123RF, (cl)Alex Cao/Photodisc/Getty Images, (cl)Shutterstock/Vorobyeva, (cr)Lauren Burke/Photographer's Choice RF/Getty Images, (cr)Clover/SuperStock, (cr)maykal/123RF, (bl)G.K. & Vikki Hart/Getty Images, (br)Lars A. Niki; **L044 Side 02** (tl)Corbis Super/Alamy, (tcl)©Ingram Publishing, (tcr)©M. Shcherbyna/Shutterstock.com, (tr)Dora Zett/Shutterstock.com, (cl)Giedre Vaitekune/123RF, (bl)Ryan McVay/Getty Images, (bcl)PhotoAlto/SuperStock, (bcl)DNY59/E+/Getty Images, (bcr)William Ryall, (br)Ilene MacDonald/Alamy; **L047 Side 01** (tl)wabeno/iStock/Getty Images, (tcl)Ingram Publishing/SuperStock, (tcr)Studiohio, (tr)Metta foto/Alamy, (l)Mark Steinmetz, (cl)Creative Control/Alamy Stock Photo, (bl)Pix11/Shutterstock.com, (bcl)McGraw-Hill Education, (bcr)Artbox/Shutterstock.com, (br)C. Zachariasen/PhotoAlto; **L049 Side 02** (tr)Comstock/Stockbyte/Getty Images; **Photo:L049 Side 02** (tl)aguirre_mar/iStock/Getty Images, (tcl)Boris Puhanic/Shutterstock.com, (tcr)Getty Images, (cl)Jeffrey Coolidge/Getty Images, (cr)Martin Damen/123RF, (bl)Mark Steinmetz/McGraw-Hill Education, (bcl)Jirsak/iStock/Getty Images, (bcr)lynx/iconotec.com/Glow Images, (br)Ingram Publishing/SuperStock; **L069 Side 02** (tl)C Squared Studios/Getty Images, (tcl)McGraw-Hill Companies Inc., Mark Steinmetz, photographer, (tcr)McGraw-Hill Education, (tr)Ildi Papp/YAY Micro/age fotostock, (cl)PhotoDisc/Getty Images, Inc., (cr)Kim DeClaire/iStock/Getty Images, (bl)C Squared Studios/Photodisc/Getty Images, (bcl)Andrey_Kuzmin/iStock/Getty Images, (br)Ingram Publishing/SuperStock, (br)Ryan McVay/Getty Images.